Mugford

Cost ana~~lysis in~~
primary he~~alth~~

A training manual for prog~~ramme~~ ~~m~~anagers

Cost analysis in primary health care

A training manual for programme managers

Edited by

Andrew Creese
Division of Strengthening of Health Services
World Health Organization
Geneva, Switzerland

&

David Parker
Office of Social Policy and Economic Analysis
United Nations Children's Fund
New York, USA

World Health Organization
Geneva
1994

WHO Library Cataloguing in Publication Data

Cost analysis in primary health care: a training manual for programme managers / edited by Andrew Creese &
David Parker.
1.Primary health care — economics 2.Costs and cost analysis — methods 3.Teaching materials
I.Creese, Andrew II.Parker, David

ISBN 92 4 154470 8   (NLM Classification: W 74)

TYPESET IN INDIA
PRINTED IN ENGLAND
93/9770-Macmillan/Clays-6500

Contents

Preface

The health sectors in many countries today are faced with severe resource constraints. Primary health care programme managers must therefore use available resources as efficiently and effectively as possible. The optimal use of resources requires clear and accurate information on resource flow, and on the impact that resources have on the quality and performance of health services.

This manual is designed to provide primary health care programme managers with guidance on how to use cost analysis and cost-effectiveness analysis as tools to achieve better understanding and management of resource flows. A firm understanding of these issues at the primary health care level represents an important step towards more equitable provision of services. The long-term sustainability of primary health care services is also dependent on the comprehensive application of cost analysis and cost-effectiveness tools and methods.

These guidelines are the result of a collaborative effort by three international organizations involved in health development, and are based on experience gained in a wide range of health programmes. They have been developed through a process of workshops and field-testing; it is expected that they will continue to evolve as further experience is gained.

It is my hope that this manual will gain wide acceptance and application, and that an improved understanding of cost issues will contribute to strengthening primary health care.

Hiroshi Nakajima,
Director-General
World Health
Organization

Acknowledgements

This manual was developed over a period of three years, through workshops and field-testing with important inputs from health programme managers in many developing countries. Financial and technical support was provided by the United Nations Children's Fund (UNICEF) and the Aga Khan Foundation. The Danish International Development Agency supported many of the workshops.

The drafting process involved a team of people with expertise in cost analysis, and in preparation and layout of training materials. Margaret Phillips, London School of Hygiene and Tropical Medicine, England, was responsible for the initial draft; Barbara McPake, London School of Hygiene and Tropical Medicine, produced most of the exercises; Charles Thube, East and Southern African Management Institute, Arusha, United Republic of Tanzania, organized a workshop to test and review the material; Robert Robertson, Mount Holyoke College, Mount Holyoke, MA, USA, made extensive revisions and produced the present text, taking into account the comments of over 30 health managers who took part in workshops in Lisbon, Portugal, and Arusha, United Republic of Tanzania. Thanks are due for the patience and cooperation of all of these persons.

Acknowledgment is also due to the other principal sources of guidance in health programme cost analysis, which have inevitably influenced thinking and practice in this area. Some of these sources, though by no means all, are listed as further reading on page 143.

Introduction

Why study costs?

Collection and analysis of data on programme costs can provide considerable useful information on primary health services of all kinds. In addition to indicating the amount of funds (from all sources) likely to be required to continue programmes, they can help you to assess the use of personnel in delivering primary health care (PHC) and the efficiency of putting supplies, transport resources and other inputs to work. These results can apply to entire programmes or to specific components of them and to comparisons of specific centres, posts and other units that deliver services. While you and your associates are estimating costs, you will probably also derive additional information of practical use—for example, vaccine wastage rates in immunization programmes.

When cost data can be related to existing or readily available information on programme performance, such as coverage of the target population by a programme or by a specific delivery site, useful assessments of efficiency in an input/output sense can be made. Similarly, while examining what you are getting for the resources you use, you can often make at least preliminary judgements about who is being helped by the health programme, which will tell you something about the equity (fairness) of the health scheme.

These and other uses of cost data are described in this manual. Training exercises are included to provide practice in collecting and interpreting data. The manual also contains guidelines about the nature of the underlying cost concepts and the principal ways of measuring them, as well as directions for the arrangement of data and the computations needed to arrive at the necessary findings. Not all users will need to read the entire contents of the manual. Thus, users interested in identifying and using unit financial costs may focus on Part A. Those interested in questions of cost recovery and sustainability will need to concentrate on Parts A and C, while those interested in an introduction to cost-effectiveness should focus on Parts A and B.

Who will use this manual?

While the manual has been prepared primarily for programme managers at national, regional, and district levels, almost any health professional can learn something from it through a short training course or by individual study. Even staff at specific delivery units, such as health centres, will find parts of it useful. Levels below the national one are all too often ignored in cost analyses and other economic assessments, but district health officers and similar officials are definitely among the target users of the manual. The community level is crucial to the management of primary health care programmes. Naturally, higher-level specialists, such as health planners who might have prior training in economics, can also put the guidelines to good use. However, no past experience or technical expertise in economics is needed.

It is likely that, as you study the manual and its exercises and follow up by doing some cost studies, your enthusiasm and confidence in examining costs and in using your findings in decision-making will increase steadily. There is a real incentive to do this: the present economic climate has produced a general scarcity of resources for the health sector in many countries, and cost analysis can help to make the best use of the limited resources available.

How this manual is organized

The manual consists of three parts containing a total of twelve modules. Part A introduces you to financial costs and provides a first look at the effectiveness of health services. Part B covers other kinds of costs and compares cost and effectiveness estimates in cost-effectiveness analysis. In Part C, several important uses of cost and cost-effectiveness data for planning and management are discussed and illustrated. At the end is a set of exercises to be used with the individual modules.

Unit financial costs

What are the costs?

Cost classification

To estimate a health programme's costs, it is necessary to classify its components. Cost elements can be broken down in several ways, as illustrated below. A good classification scheme depends on the needs of the particular situation or problem, but there are three essential elements:

- It must be relevant to the particular situation.
- The classes (categories) must not overlap.
- The classes chosen must cover all possibilities.

Economists define cost as the value of resources used to produce something, including a specific health service or a set of services (as in a health programme). Resources used for PHC programmes can be described in many different ways. For example, a diarrhoeal diseases control programme might be described as using the following resources: personnel, money from external sources and mass media. These categories are well defined and their meaning is clear. However, they do not constitute a very useful way of thinking about the resources used in this programme. The main problem is that the categories overlap; money from external sources can be used to pay for personnel, and personnel are likely to be involved in mass media operations. If we add up the value of these three categories, they may well come to more than the total cost of the programme.

One reason why the categories above are difficult to use is that they confuse different dimensions of resources, mixing activities (in this case "mass media") with sources ("money from external sources") and physical inputs ("personnel"). Obviously, several different classification schemes are involved here. These and others need to be looked at separately, starting with the most basic resource inputs. Examples of resource inputs include personnel, supplies and equipment.

Classification by inputs

This type of classification of costs is useful and widely applicable. It groups inputs into categories in which the elements have recognizably similar characteristics, for example vehicles, personnel and supplies. If used properly, this scheme has many merits, including the following:

- It involves a manageable number of categories, and these categories are general enough to be applied to any health programme.

- It distinguishes two important categories of resources, those that are used up in the course of a year and are usually purchased regularly (i.e. recurrent costs) and those that last longer than one year, such as buildings, vehicles and equipment (i.e. capital costs).
- It focuses attention on the operating (recurrent) costs of investments in vehicles, equipment and buildings by making these into distinct categories.

Any classification requires basic definitions and avoidance of confusion. For example, more than one word can be used to refer to a single group of resources. "Manpower" and "personnel" are two such words. Secondly, there are differences in the degree of detail; "personnel" can be further subdivided into doctors, nurses, administrators and technicians. For a practical exercise in identifying resource inputs, see exercise 1A on page 96. Then return to this point in the module.

A scheme for classifying costs by inputs (with examples of each category) is shown in the chart below.

Classification of costs by inputs

Capital costs

- Vehicles: bicycles, motorcycles, four-wheel-drive vehicles, trucks
- Equipment: refrigerators, sterilizers, manufacturing machinery, scales, other equipment with a unit cost (price) of $100 or more
- Buildings, space: health centres, hospitals, training schools, administrative offices, storage facilities
- Training, nonrecurrent: training activities for health personnel that occur only once or rarely
- Social mobilization, nonrecurrent: social mobilization activities, e.g. promotion, publicity campaigns, that occur only once or rarely

Recurrent costs

- Personnel (all types): supervisors, health workers, administrators, technicians, consultants, casual labour
- Supplies: drugs, vaccines, syringes, small equipment (unit cost of less than $100)
- Vehicles, operation & maintenance: petrol, diesel, lubricants, tyres, spare parts, registration, insurance
- Buildings, operation & maintenance: electricity, water, heating, fuel, telephone, telex, insurance, cleaning, painting, repairs to electrical supply/appliances, plumbing, roofing and heating
- Training, recurrent (e.g. short in-service courses)
- Social mobilization: operating costs
- Other operating costs not included above

To apply the recommended chart of input categories, see exercise 1B, page 96.

Some possible secondary classifications

Describing the resources used in terms of physical inputs, as we have done above, is one way of dividing them up. However, it is not the only way. Resources have other characteristics that are important. There are four other characteristics that you might find helpful in describing and assessing the costs of your programme. They are usually less important than the inputs scheme, and are explained briefly below.

Classification by function/activity

The first of the secondary classifications involves the kind of activity or function for which the resources are used. A maternal and child health (MCH) programme, for example, encompasses a wide range of activities, such as tetanus toxoid vaccinations for pregnant women, prenatal care, supervision of deliveries, and immunization and weighing of children. For each of these activities, groups of physical inputs are required. For example, infant weighing requires personnel to do the weighing and record the results, scales, tables, charts, building space and possibly vehicles.

To practise using these ideas on functions or activities, see exercise 1C, page 97.

The activities mentioned above for MCH are a limited set. They include only the service provision activities. Did you remember to include in your list the essential activities that support and complement them? Examples that you are likely to find in most health programmes include:

- training,
- supervision,
- management,
- monitoring and evaluation,
- logistics and transport.

In most cases, identifying the different functional components is straightforward. However, it may be easy to miss some functions that are handled separately from the rest of the programme, either institutionally or financially. For example, the communications aspect of your programme may be funded or implemented outside the Ministry of Health and could be overlooked. If you are looking at the whole health sector and not just at single programmes, the functional breakdown may be in terms of preventive or curative programmes or by type of institution—hospital, health centre or staff training institution. For PHC, distinguishing among institutions, especially hospitals, is probably unnecessary.

There is one other thing to be careful about when estimating the costs of multiple-activity programmes. You will have to allocate resources that are shared among the activities so that each is charged only for its proper share. This is especially important for personnel in some cases. Accounting methods for dealing with such allocations are covered in Module 4.

Classification by level

Another way of dividing up resources is according to the level at which they are used. For most health programmes there is an obvious hierarchy of operations. In a national programme, for example, some resources are used at the central or national level while others are used at the provincial, regional or district level. And some are further decentralized to health facilities or to the community, village or household level. You may be responsible for, or involved in, a national programme at the central level or at any of the other levels. Where several levels are involved, you must decide for each cost analysis whether you want to classify the results by level, i.e. according to where the output takes place.

Classification by source

The source (provider) of the resources is another very important characteristic. Contributors may include the Ministry of Health, other national government departments, local government bodies, international donors, bilateral donors, independent nongovernmental charitable or private organizations, community groups and individuals.

You might wish to break down your costs according to source (perhaps tied to specific activities or inputs) for financial reporting, including reporting to donors, or for predicting calls on national funds in the future. From such data, you could also estimate the "multiplier effect" of external assistance, which shows whether a boost in total health spending is associated with the aid. This kind of classification is quite straightforward in principle.

Classification by currency

Closely associated with the source of the resources is the type of currency required to purchase those resources. Bilateral and international donors, for example, very often supply goods and services that need to be purchased in foreign currency (i.e. foreign to the recipient). The distinction between resources requiring domestic currency and those requiring foreign currency is an important one, particularly in those developing countries where there is a shortage of foreign (or convertible) currency. Donor contributions are a way of easing foreign exchange shortages. However, donors may not be able to continue their support indefinitely, and it is useful to know what foreign currency burden would then fall on the government.

In a few cost studies, the initial estimates are adjusted to correct any distortions in exchange rates caused by artificially set official rates. You might need a classification of findings by type of currency to make such adjustments, along with some expert advice. See exercise 1D, page 98, for more on classification by type of currency, and see Module 7 for further discussion of foreign exchange.

The topic of exchange rates raises a question that goes beyond classifications: when and how should cost values in a local currency be converted to some kind of international medium, such as the United States dollar? For internal uses of cost data, such a conversion should not be necessary, and some countries' studies have been left entirely in the national currency. However, if the results of an analysis of programme costs are to be compared with those of programmes in other countries, conversion to a common monetary measure will be necessary. To avoid possible errors from using an official exchange rate, you should consult economic specialists or officials of other agencies—for example, the Ministry of Finance or the central bank.

Conclusion

If you look at small enough pieces of the resource input picture, it is possible to describe each resource (and to estimate its cost) both in terms of the type (category) of physical input and in terms of any one of four secondary classifications, i.e. function or activity, level at which resources are used, source or contributor, and currency.

You should be aware of these distinct features of the resources used in your programme. Avoid mixing different characteristics in the same list, or you may have problems deciding how to categorize some resources. For example, if you have personnel (a physical input) and mass media (an activity) in the same list, where do you classify staff who are involved in mass media activities? The danger is that you may count things twice, or perhaps even forget them altogether.

Sometimes, it may be justifiable to include an activity within a list of inputs. If one activity is clearly separate from the others, both financially and administratively, it may be easier not to attempt to break it down into its component physical inputs, but merely to record the total cost. For example, training and social mobilization activities are treated above as categories of inputs and included along with personnel, vehicles and the like. When this is done, it is assumed that all the resources required for the activity (e.g. personnel and vehicles) are included in that category (e.g. training) and not under the separate categories of personnel, vehicles, and so forth. Thus, the full cost of all inputs used for training is estimated and used as the value for that category.

To conclude this module and check your understanding of the main points, see exercises 1E, 1F, and 1G, pages 98–101.

Using cost data

The introduction to this manual describes some uses of cost information. This module tells you more about the usefulness of the results of cost analyses. As you will see, they can be helpful in meeting requirements for accountability and judging (and promoting) programme efficiency as well as achieving other goals.

Accountability—keeping track

It should come as no surprise that, as an employee of the government or of a nongovernmental organization (NGO), you are accountable to your employers (and they, in turn, are usually accountable to the public) for your expenditure or the resources you use. To meet the obligations of accountability, you need, at the very least, to:

- know how you have spent the finances available to you; and
- ensure that the money you control has been spent as intended.

All this might seem like a simple exercise in financial housekeeping, but failure to acknowledge its consequences can have unfortunate results. No one can just *assume* that budgeted funds have been spent exactly—no more and no less—and that they have been used properly. Most government and private organizations have mechanisms to protect their funds from misuse and waste. As well as responding to questions from higher levels of the administration, you can do several useful things at the programme or district level to achieve greater accountability.

Take a moment to consider the kinds of accounting mechanisms that you have in your programme for keeping track of expenditure and minimizing waste and misuse. Which of these mechanisms appear to work well and which poorly? Now we will show you some specific steps to help you to achieve accountability, starting with a look at your budget.

At the level of the overall programme, the budget provides guidelines on how resources should be used. The budget is a document which sets out in general terms how much money should be spent on different inputs or activities. It describes planned expenditure over a defined period—usually one year, some-times longer.

Even if you ignore this plan, others will not. Failure to stick reasonably closely to your budget is likely to cause you considerable problems. If your expenditure begins to exceed the budget, you will need to look for additional resources. This can be a time-consuming and frustrating task. And if it is not successful, the effectiveness of your programme may be seriously jeopardized; for example, if a malaria programme cannot afford to buy drugs, it is not likely to be very successful in controlling malaria.

You may also have problems if you fail to spend the entire amount budgeted. The Ministry of Finance or other authority that controls budget allocations may automatically reduce your future budgets on the assumption that you will be unable to use all the resources you have requested.

For all these reasons, it is desirable for budget and expenditure to be closely linked. It is, therefore, essential to keep track of what you are spending throughout the year. If you find that expenditure on a particular item is too slow, or that the budget allowance is being consumed too rapidly, you may be able to take appropriate action early to avoid a major mismatch between budget and expenditure. You might derive some guidance from past experience. Are your budget and expenditure better or more poorly matched now than in previous years?

There are several possible explanations for a mismatch between budget and expenditure. One is that the budget is poorly prepared: perhaps it reflects an inadequate understanding of the resources required to achieve particular stated objectives, so that it simply does not allow sufficient resources to achieve them. This may be because the total allocation is inadequate, or because the distribution of allocated resources is wrong (e.g. too much for salaries but not enough for vehicle fuel) and the budget is not flexible enough to be realistic. Either way, the manager is in the impossible situation of attempting to reconcile overambitious objectives with inadequate resources. This situation is all too often the manager's own fault, since he or she usually has the opportunity to comment on, if not design, the budget. (Module 10 discusses procedures for preparing a good budget.)

Another possible explanation is that the programme itself is being poorly implemented: resources are being squandered, used inefficiently, even diverted to other uses. Finally, the mismatch may be due to unexpected changes, such as a sudden devaluation of the national currency, a rise in the price of a major input, or a natural disaster.

In order to identify possible causes of mismatch between budget and expenditure, look at your expenditure in detail. First of all, study each major category of input. You might notice, for example, that expenditure on personnel has been much higher than allowed for in the budget, and realize that this can be attributed to an unexpected increase in wage rates. Or you may note that there has been underspending on equipment and discover that there have been problems with importing particular items of equipment, or perhaps a shortage of foreign exchange. Perhaps you may realize that the amount you allowed for fuel was inadequate, given the number of vehicles you operate.

If your budget is also broken down by functions (activities), you can analyse each functional budget in the same way. Did any particular function (e.g. training) account for the total budget being overspent or underspent? You might also have separate budgets for different levels in your programme (national, regional, district), or for each contributor to your programme, or for local and foreign currency. You can examine each set of budgets to find out where to focus your attention when trying to improve the situation next year.

In other words, there are many possible steps you can take to interpret a situation in which the budgeted and the actual expenditure are too far apart. For practice in interpreting and remedying such a mismatch, see exercise 2A, page 102. Return to this point after completing the exercise.

Assessing efficiency

A health programme or service delivery unit is more efficient when it provides more beneficial effects from the use of a given set of resources. Details of effects as well as costs are found in later modules. Here, the aim is to allow health officials to make some judgements about efficiency by examining fairly simple cost presentations. They are based on "cost profiles", which show each input in terms of an absolute value and as a percentage of the total cost. (Similar profiles might break the total down by activity or by level.) An example of a cost profile is shown below.

Input category	Annual cost (currency)	Share of total cost (%)
Capital		
Vehicles	5000	10
Equipment	5000	10
Buildings, space	5000	10
Training, nonrecurrent	0	
Social mobilization, nonrecurrent	0	
Subtotal, capital	15 000	30
Recurrent		
Personnel	20 000	40
Supplies	5000	10
Vehicles, operation & maintenance	5000	10
Buildings, operation & maintenance	1000	2
Training, recurrent	0	
Social mobilization, recurrent	0	
Other operating inputs	4000	8
Subtotal, recurrent	35 000	70
Total	50 000	100

You can use cost profiles in two different, but related, ways. *Firstly,* cost profiles highlight the categories that you should focus on in further studies of efficiency; the larger the cost category, the more attention it should be given, because the potential for savings is greater. For example, in the above case, if it were possible to reduce personnel costs by a certain percentage, this would have a much larger impact on total costs than the same percentage reduction in any other input. A 20% reduction in personnel costs would reduce total costs by 8% (20% of 40%), but the same percentage reduction in vehicles as a capital input would reduce total costs by only 2% (20% of 10%). The relative sizes of the categories might also tell you how much effort to put into estimating their costs. However, you must be careful. The inputs that seem to have the most potential for cost reduction are not necessarily those that should be cut. They may be the inputs that are already being used most efficiently, so that cutting back on them may have a drastic effect on the outputs. Even if they are not being used efficiently, it may be difficult to change them. For example, salaries may be an important input and one that is not being used optimally, but altering staff arrangements may be impossible in the short term. Nevertheless, despite these necessary qualifications, identifying the major inputs is a useful starting point for exploring the efficiency of a programme.

The *second* way you can use cost profiles is to compare the profiles of similar units. It can reasonably be assumed that similar units should have similar cost profiles. The units may be different health centres or different geographical areas, such as districts. Major differences in the cost profiles of similar units should prompt you to investigate further. Significant differences indicate that there may be ways of restructuring some units to improve their efficiency. In other words, you need to do further studies to establish the reasons behind any cost profile differences before you can draw any firm conclusions about what action might be appropriate.

Exercise 2B, page 103, gives you an introduction to the use of comparative cost profiles for districts. *After* you have done it, return here for some possible answers, including policies to promote greater efficiency.

One explanation for the differences in spending on drugs by the centres in exercise 2B could be that the staff of the health centre with a high expenditure on drugs are overprescribing (prescribing drugs that are unnecessary, or in larger quantities than necessary, or drugs that are more expensive than necessary). Or this centre may have a high wastage rate because of problems of storage or theft. A look at the drugs inventory, the storage facilities and the treatment records of that centre should show you which of these is the problem. Improvements in prescription habits and drug management would be necessary to remedy these problems.

A second, equally plausible, explanation is that the difference in drug expenditure is not the result of inefficiency at the high-expenditure health centre:

the *other* centres, far from being efficient, may in fact be unable to treat all their patients adequately, because of an irregular supply of drugs. Drug inventory checks would readily establish whether this is the explanation. The appropriate remedy would be to increase the reliability of drug supplies to those centres, which would obviously involve remedial action above the health centre level.

A third possible explanation is that there are differences in the pattern of disease, or the cost of transporting drugs, or the size of the population served which explain why one health centre has relatively high drug costs. The observed cost differences may thus be justified by the circumstances, in which case there may be little that can, or should, be done to improve efficiency.

This line of analysis points to the need for preparation of cost profiles for many or all of the service delivery units, such as health centres, within a district. Likewise, programme profiles should be drawn up within each district. If a programme covers more than one district, a total programme profile will consist of the sum of the relevant programmes in the districts. That probably sounds like a large task, but in fact it should not be too burdensome. The possible benefits in the form of greater efficiency, and better health of the population, make the effort worth while.

Cost analysis to improve efficiency does not stop with the use of profiles. It will also be helpful to calculate average (unit) costs, for example, cost per patient visit to a centre or cost per vaccine dose in an immunization programme. There, too, examination of "outliers"—that is, the centres with the highest or the lowest cost values—can lead to useful policies. Later in this manual, you will see examples of estimating average costs and of applying the results in practice.

Assessing equity

Equity means fairness: for instance, equal availability or use of health services for everyone who needs them. The distribution of health resources is one very important indicator of equity and examination of this is a necessary first step towards more detailed analysis. If one district receives twice as much of your programme expenditure as another, there might well be a case for better balance of resources on grounds of equity. Of course, total cost is not a very helpful guide. One of the major determinants of cost is the number of people served: the district using more resources may simply serve many more people. A better measure is the cost per person (that is, the total cost divided by the number of people in the target population). When analysing the equity of health services, you may need to take into account services provided by other organizations, such as other government programmes, NGOs and other private providers of primary care.

The comparisons you can usefully make are between people served by different facilities or in different geographical areas. You might wish to focus on urban vs rural or on income differences; variations in per capita expenditure between different ethnic groups or other sectors of the population might also be worth examining in some cases.

You can begin to make judgements about the equity of your programme or another set of PHC activities by doing exercise 2C, page 104. After you have tried that exercise, return here for some possible answers to the last question, concerning differences between districts.

If you identify major differences between two districts in the cost per person served, there are several possible explanations. Suppose that the cost per head in district A is much higher than that in district B. It may be that:

- The authorities are aiming for equity in the nature of the services delivered. To do this they have to spend more per head in district A, because the highly dispersed population and the rugged terrain there make it more expensive to deliver the same level of services as district B is receiving.
- The authorities are aiming for equity in the nature of the services delivered, but there is much more waste in district A, which makes it more expensive.
- The authorities are attempting to ensure that both districts have equally good health. Because the population in district A is less healthy than in district B (because of the terrain, the type of employment, genetic factors, the age structure, etc.), it makes more demands on the health facilities and thus requires more services per person.
- The authorities are trying to guarantee the maximum *improvement* in health from their investment. They are putting more resources per head into district A, either because it is cheaper to provide services there or because the population is less healthy.
- The authorities are vulnerable to the stronger influence and lobbying power of district A. District A is favoured politically and has more health resources put into it, although there may be no significant differences in population or terrain.

Clearly it is important to decide which of these explanations is valid before you take action. You might consider that the first three explanations are acceptable, but you would perhaps wish to challenge discrimination on political grounds or because of the difficulty of providing services in some areas.

In the final section of this module ("Tables for presenting and analysing expenditure data"), there is a suggested layout of a table for arranging data by district to judge geographical equity.

Assessing priorities

At least in the case of vertical or special-purpose programmes, e.g. the Expanded Programme on Immunization (EPI), the value of the resources devoted to a programme is some measure of the national priority accorded to it. You may find it useful to know what is being spent on your programme in comparison with other programmes. Are the results compatible with previously stated priorities? You may be able to use the results to negotiate for further funding. Some of the questions to consider are these:

- What is government expenditure per person on your programme?
- How does it compare with government expenditure per head on other health programmes?
- Has expenditure per head on your programme increased or decreased since last year? Why?
- What percentage of total government health expenditure is directed towards your programme? Has this been increasing or decreasing over time? (You might need some help in finding the answers to these questions.)

The answers to all these questions can then be related to the priority that the government claims to give your programme. Planning documents and policy statements are useful sources of information about stated priorities. You could also put these questions to other, nongovernmental contributors to your programme, and use the results to encourage contributors to "put their money where their mouth is".

Making cost projections

Knowing what you are spending on your existing programme can also be very important for judging future costs. Expenditure is not a self-contained item; what you spend this year is likely to affect what you will need to spend next year. In particular, expenditure on capital goods generally implies a need for continued funding of the associated recurrent costs if the capital item is to be used properly. By studying past relationships between the cost of capital items and their associated operating and maintenance costs, you will be in a better position to estimate the future financial requirements of your programme.

You can also use your experience of what a certain kind of programme actually costs to estimate what a similar programme might cost in the future. Module 10 tells you more about these applications, including how to estimate future costs and use the results.

Considering cost recovery

The cost of a health service or programme is one of the pieces of information that must be known if a country is considering introducing user charges (fees imposed on patients or on the agency supporting them) as one of the sources of financing.

The aim might be to recover the cost of drugs or (much less likely) of all recurrent inputs, or the full cost of the service. If, for example, you are required to cover all local recurrent costs through fees, then the average local recurrent cost per unit of service will be a good guide to the price you should set.

Especially if the policy-makers of a programme are attempting to recover more than minor recurrent costs, they will need to consider the effect of user fees on the demand for services. A fall in demand may lead to an increase in average cost per beneficiary. (Even if the aim is to recover only a small portion of total costs, the price charged might affect the quantity of services demanded.)

Of course, equity should also be taken into account, in terms of the patients' ability to pay for care. Assessment of this is sometimes a difficult task that goes well beyond cost estimation. (There is further discussion of this point in Module 11.)

Tables for presenting and analysing expenditure data

To summarize and conclude this module, a number of tables and exercises are presented. The tables are to help you to analyse the costs of your programme, using the results to judge efficiency, equity and priorities, to project costs into the future, and to consider cost recovery. (Corresponding practical problems are found in exercise 2D, page 105.) Below each table are some important questions that the table should help you to answer.

The tables below and the corresponding exercises, when completed for local (community) level PHC activities, will necessarily lack some details available for multiple-level or national programmes. And specific items, such as the sources of support, will be somewhat different. Nevertheless, the general approach to analysis indicated by the tables can be helpful to local officials as well as to others.

Table 2.1. Comparison of budget and expenditure

Input	Budget (currency)	Expenditure (currency)	Cost profile (expenditure as % of budget)
Capital			
Vehicles			
Equipment			
Buildings, space			
Training, nonrecurrent			
Social mobilization, nonrecurrent			
Subtotal, capital			
Recurrent			
Personnel			
Supplies			
Vehicles, operation & maintenance			
Buildings, operation & maintenance			
Training, recurrent			
Social mobilization, recurrent			
Subtotal, recurrent			
Total			

Did total expenditure keep within the budget? Compared with previous years, are budgets and expenditures matched?

Which inputs were overspent and which were underspent?

What percentage of total expenditure was on capital? What are the recurrent cost implications of this capital expenditure?

On which inputs was expenditure greatest? (These should be a focus for further efficiency studies.)

How does the expenditure per head compare with that of other programmes? Does this reflect stated priorities?

Table 2.2 Expenditure by source of support (contributor)

	Donors		Ministry of Health		Other government departments		Total	
Input	Currency	%	Currency	%	Currency	%	Currency	%
Capital								
Vehicles								
Equipment								
Buildings, space								
Training, nonrecurrent								
Social mobilization, nonrecurrent								
Subtotal, capital								
Recurrent								
Personnel								
Supplies								
Vehicles, operation & maintenance								
Buildings, operation & maintenance								
Training, recurrent								
Social mobilization, recurrent								
Other operating inputs								
Subtotal, recurrent								
Total								

What percentage of total costs is provided by donors? How does this compare with previous years?

Which inputs are more dependent than others on outside donors?

Table 2.3 Expenditure by type of currency

Currency input	Donors		Ministry of Health		Other government departments		Total	
	Currency	%	Currency	%	Currency	%	Currency	%
Foreign exchange								
Capital inputs								
Recurrent inputs								
Subtotal								
Local currency								
Capital inputs								
Recurrent inputs								
Subtotal								
Total								

What percentage of total expenditure involves foreign exchange?

Which contributors provide most of the foreign exchange?

Are capital or recurrent inputs more dependent on foreign exchange?

Table 2.4 Expenditure by function (activity)

Input	Training Currency %	Management Currency %	Delivery Currency %	Education Currency %	Total Currency %
Capital					
Vehicles					
Equipment					
Buildings, space					
Training, nonrecurrent					
Social mobilization, nonrecurrent					
Subtotal, capital					
Recurrent					
Personnel					
Supplies					
Vehicles, operation & maintenance					
Buildings, operation & maintenance					
Training, recurrent					
Social mobilization, recurrent					
Other operating inputs					
Subtotal, recurrent					
Total					

What functions are overspent/underspent?

Which functions are most capital-intensive (i.e. require a high percentage of capital inputs)?

On what function is expenditure highest?

Does that function give you the most scope for improving efficiency? Why/why not?

Table 2.5 Expenditure by level

Input	National administration		Regional administration		District administration		Health centre		Hospital		Total	
	Currency	%	Currency	%	Currency	%	Currency	%	Currency	%	Currency	%
Capital												
Vehicles												
Equipment												
Buildings, space												
Training, nonrecurrent												
Social mobilization, nonrecurrent												
Subtotal, capital												

Recurrent

Personnel

Supplies

Vehicles, operation
& maintenance

Buildings, operation
& maintenance

Training, recurrent

Social mobilization,
recurrent

Other operating
inputs

Subtotal, recurrent

Total

At which level are most of the costs incurred?

At which level is the percentage of expenditure on capital inputs the highest?

Table 2.6 Expenditure by district*

	District A		District B		District C		District D		Total	
Input	Currency	%	Currency	%	Currency	%	Currency	%	Currency	%
Capital										
Vehicles										
Equipment										
Buildings, space										
Training, nonrecurrent										
Social mobilization, nonrecurrent										
Subtotal, capital										
Recurrent										
Personnel										
Supplies										
Vehicles, operation & maintenance										
Buildings, operation & maintenance										
Training, recurrent										
Social mobilization, recurrent										
Other operating inputs										
Subtotal, recurrent										
Total										

*Instead of districts, other subdivisions might be used, such as health centres or other delivery units within a district or within a programme.

If budgets are also kept by district, check which districts overspent and which underspent.

Are there any districts where the cost profiles are significantly different? What might account for this?

In which districts are the costs per head lowest? What might account for this?

MODULE 3

Planning the study

In Module 1, the cost of a health service is defined as the value of the resource inputs used to produce that service. Up to this point in the manual, the cost of an input has been treated as though it were equivalent to the expenditure required to put it to use. In practice, expenditure figures may need to be adjusted and supplemented by additional information in order to yield true economic costs (see Module 7). For now, though, the focus continues to be on expenditure. One point from Module 2 deserves to be repeated here: it is *actual* expenditure and not simply the budgeted (expected or hoped for) value that counts as cost.

This module provides guidance on planning the scope of the cost study and identifying sources of information for the data collection phase. Data collection is considered further in Module 4, where cost calculations are discussed.

Setting the scope of the cost analysis

Before you start measuring costs, you must be quite clear about the scope of the programme or set of services that you are costing. A good way to clarify exactly what you are intending to cost is to use the classifications presented in Module 1 as a checklist. First consider all the functions (activities) involved in your programme, record them, and note any that you intend to exclude. Do the same thing with the contributors to your programme and for the different levels at which your programme functions. Within the limits defined by the functions, levels and contributors, elaborate on the types of physical input used to produce the services in your programme. You should attempt to specify all inputs, preferably using the categories described in Modules 1 and 2. As a general practice, it would also be wise to be as comprehensive as possible in terms of functions, levels and sources of funds, although for some purposes exclusions will be appropriate. For example, you may be interested only in the costs incurred by the government (i.e. a certain contributor) within one district (i.e. a certain level) for the educational component of a nutrition programme (i.e. a particular function). This clearly sets the limits of the analysis.

Your decision on scope will be governed by the questions you are asking. They, in turn, will be determined by the range of your responsibilities and the circumstances of the programme. Module 9 gives more details about how to decide what the scope of the cost study should be in order to answer questions about cost-effectiveness.

Deciding on the time period

Usually, you should attempt to measure the costs incurred over one full year. This is likely to be consistent with the records of most types of relevant data, such as expenditure on personnel and services provided. A one-year period avoids any distortions that might be caused by seasonal effects. Occasionally, limitations of information, e.g. for a new programme, or of study time might make it necessary to choose a shorter period. If you study costs for less than one year, you will probably need to discuss ways of avoiding serious distortions with other knowledgeable persons.

You should choose the most recent year for which cost data are likely to be available. If the year chosen is too far in the past, important information may be lost. If the year is too recent, some routinely collected statistics may not yet be available.

If you are doing a cost-effectiveness analysis, you also need to be aware of any limitations on availability of effectiveness data. Usually you would collect cost and effectiveness data for the same period, since the effects recommended for measurement in Modules 5 and 9 follow almost immediately from the input of resources. (There can be exceptions to that rule.)

Sometimes the financial year (the period for which routinely collected expenditure data are summarized) is not the same as the calendar year (the period for which effectiveness statistics are likely to be aggregated). If this is the case, see whether it is possible to obtain disaggregated data for each month covering costs or effectiveness, so that you can construct either annual effectiveness data for the financial year or expenditure figures for the calendar year. Otherwise, it may be necessary to use cost and effectiveness data from slightly different periods.

Selecting a sample

With a programme that has a large number of dispersed delivery units (such as a district-level or national-level PHC programme that operates through many health centres), it may not be possible to do a complete costing. This is certainly true if the routinely collected statistics are not adequate and someone has to visit each unit. Even within one health centre, you may not be able to measure every input. For example, it would be practically impossible to record the amount of time devoted by staff members to a programme by monitoring their movements every day of the year. In these situations, it is necessary to choose a sample of units from the total population. "Population" is a term that statisticians use in general to describe the total of all possible observations. It might include, for example, days in the year, health centres in the district or potential patients in the target group. You must be explicit about the base from which your sample is drawn. If any units are deliberately excluded from the original population, the nature of and reasons for the exclusion should be stated.

There are several ways in which you can make your selection. Usually, in taking a sample, you are not just interested in the particular units you select. You wish to be able to draw conclusions about the population as a whole. If this is the case, there are certain rules you must follow. Statisticians have devised many different approaches to satisfy the conditions necessary to allow valid conclusions to be drawn about the population from samples. Four of these approaches are described below. For each of them, the size of the sample drawn will influence the degree to which inevitable statistical variation will affect the confidence to be placed in the estimate for the whole population. Disregarding expense and other problems, the larger the sample, the greater the confidence (i.e. the smaller the range of probable error). Another factor is the extent of variation among units of the population; smaller variations permit a smaller sample size. You might wish to consult a statistician about these matters.

One of the customary approaches to selection is *random sampling*. This is a good technique to use if you can feasibly list (and number) all the elements of the entire population and if there are no subgroups you are particularly interested in. You could, for instance, use it in selecting health centres within a district. Having decided on the sample size, you would select the required number of units at random from a numbered list, using a table of random numbers.

Systematic sampling is a second approach. It is easier to use than simple random sampling, and is most useful when there are large numbers in the population (say, patients attending a hospital). The procedure is as follows:

- Obtain a list of all the units (n) (in no systematic order) from which the sample is to be selected.
- Decide on the size of the sample (s).
- Calculate the ratio n/s ($= k$). Select every kth item on the list, starting at any point. For example, say you want a sample of 50 patients (i.e. $s = 50$) out of 2000 attending the clinic in a year (i.e. $n = 2000$). Then $k = 2000/50 = 40$, and you would then select every 40th patient. If s does not divide exactly into n, e.g. $k = 40.54$, then round k up or down to the nearest whole number.

If you were interested in the health centre costs of a PHC programme in the country as a whole, studying a random (or stratified) sample would probably require a lot of travelling and effort, since these units are likely to be widely dispersed. An alternative approach is first to select a sample of districts and then to look at the health centre costs only in those districts. This is called *cluster sampling*. It gives less valid results than pure random sampling, but can have major logistic advantages. You must first select a random sample to determine the clusters (in this case, districts) to be studied. Then, in the selected clusters, either select all the units (health centres) or a random sample of them.

A fourth approach with a formal statistical basis is *stratified sampling*. You may wish to ensure that you include units with particular characteristics in your sample (e.g. health centres in both rural and urban areas), so that you can compare them. To do this, first divide the total population (in this case, all the health centres) into subgroups (urban and rural); then take a random or systematic sample or even a clustered sample in each subgroup.

While the mathematical merits of the above approaches are well known to specialists, there are situations when a less formal, but more practical, sampling technique might be used, which may be referred to as *judgement sampling*. In a substantial number of practical cases, barriers to statistical sampling might exist, for example excessive costs or limited cooperation from staff in specific delivery units. When one of these problems occurs, random sampling may not be possible, and you may need to use your own judgement to select a reasonably typical group of units for study. The practical advantages of this method are evident, but the inability to draw general conclusions about the entire population on a formal statistical basis is a clear drawback to the use of a judgement sample. It is offered as a less than ideal, but occasionally practical, approach to the task of choosing your sample.

To test your understanding of some of the points in this section, see exercise 3A, page 114.

Drawing up an itinerary and checklists

Usually it is difficult to get reliable cost data, especially on personnel, buildings and equipment, without visiting the site where the resources are being used. Most PHC programmes function at many levels, from health centres up to national headquarters. Some of the data may be centralized, but it is often necessary to confirm or elaborate on them by visiting more peripheral levels. You will need to prepare an itinerary before you start data collection.

In general, it is best to start at the most central level relevant to the activity you are costing. This would be the national headquarters if you were studying the costs of a national PHC programme, or the district headquarters if the district were your area of study. For studies within hospitals, or production plants, your first contacts should be the chief administrator and the finance officer. At this level you can:

- Determine the costs incurred by the programme at that level. These will need to be allocated (distributed) among various levels or delivery units if the higher-level resources are shared (the ways of handling allocations are explained in Module 4).

- Collect data on costs incurred at lower levels which, if available at the national level at all, are likely to be of better quality and more rapidly collected (e.g. vaccine use and prices in the case of an immunization programme).
- Obtain information about the number and kinds of units performing the programme activities, which you will need in order to select a sample, as well as other information to help you describe the programme.

You should then proceed to the next level down (say, the regional headquarters if you were studying the costs of a national programme) and collect the same kind of information. Once you have collected all the data from the field, at all levels, you should return to the central level. This is important in order to verify data, seek reactions to your preliminary conclusions and fill in any gaps identified. The procedure should be repeated at each level within the programme you are costing, as far as time allows. For example, in each district you should start at the district office, then visit health centres, and afterwards return to the district headquarters.

Some costs may be estimated from information collected at more than one level. For example, information about the use of staff time is likely to be learned from lower levels, while information about standard salary schedules and fringe benefits for the same staff is usually best obtained at the national level.

In the process of data collection, several ground rules should be observed. Three especially important ones are:

- Collect the information at the highest level at which it is available (if it is of reasonable quality) to minimize study time and expense.
- Be careful to avoid counting the same cost element (input) twice ("double-counting") when you have obtained data at more than one level (for example, when staffing or salary figures have been provided at both the delivery-unit and higher levels).
- Put your greatest efforts into finding (and using) information on the largest input categories rather than the smaller, less important categories (such as supplies and building operation in most programmes). The latter can often be handled by rough calculations, perhaps based on rules of thumb, such as assuming operating costs of buildings to be equal to a certain percentage of their annual capital costs.

For each level, you should draw up a checklist of the information you need to collect. This is particularly important if returning to collect forgotten data would be difficult. If you do not know in advance where the data can be found, draw up a single comprehensive list that can be checked at each level. Among other things, it should include detailed examples for every category of input in the list and tables shown in Modules 1 and 2.

Locating information sources

The type and location of many sources of information needed for cost analysis will be obvious to you. However, the nature and quality of some other sources may warrant a brief explanation here. You will no doubt be able to draw on the assistance of other health officials and on your own experience to supplement the information given here.

The first step in estimating the financial cost of your programme is to consult existing records of expenditure or accounts that document actual *spending*, rather than budget records that refer only to planned expenditure. Expenditure records are normally compiled and available centrally—at the district, regional or national level—and provide a convenient source of data. Some data will be found only at lower levels, perhaps even at the delivery units themselves.

Unfortunately, existing expenditure records are often unsatisfactory for some or all of the following reasons:

- Records are often compiled some time after the actual expenditure, or are not compiled at all, because they can be difficult and costly to maintain, especially at the lower levels. They may not clearly separate expenditure under different programmes, and may not be coded accurately by category of input. The groups of inputs may not be the ones you need; for example, there may be a single category "fuel" when you would like to distinguish fuel for vehicles from fuel for other purposes.
- Certain inputs pose special problems because an excessive volume of records is kept on them for fiscal accountability purposes (this is especially true of drugs).
- An information system that depends on passing data down from higher to lower levels initially and back up to the higher ones again for final reporting inevitably creates errors.

Despite these potential limitations, you have no alternative but to use these records for expenditure and other data needed in cost studies. It is possible to improve the design of some records and to make reasonably simple checks of their general accuracy. For further consideration of expenditure records, see exercise 3B, page 114.

If expenditure records are not gathered routinely in a format that is useful for analysis, you will need to collect some additional data. This generally means finding out the quantities of resources purchased and the prices paid for them. For example, if you wish to know the expenditure of an immunization programme on syringes, but the expenditure records do not provide sufficient detail, you will need to find out the number of syringes used during the year (say, 50 000) and the price of each (say, $0.20) in order to derive the total cost of syringes (50 000 × 0.20 = $10 000).

Generally speaking, much better records—for example, reports of physical inventories—are kept of capital items (which are more expensive) than of recurrent items. Expenditure records will usually indicate purchases of vehicles and equipment, and perhaps buildings. Buildings pose problems, though, because of the difference between original and replacement costs and the significance of inflation; in fact, their costs are often better estimated by their rental value, as explained in Module 4. You may need to supplement your reading of expenditure records by interviewing staff to obtain enough details about items that were purchased specifically for your programme. You may also need to consult purchasing orders and inventories. The ways in which information on capital inputs as well as recurrent ones can be used in cost calculations are explained in Module 4.

Calculating costs

Module 3 described briefly how to collect information on resource inputs to a health programme or a specific service. When recording data needed for calculation of costs, you should consider the following:

- If you believe that most of the cost values you have obtained are quite accurate, specify data to the smallest monetary unit (e.g. $0.01) and do not round to a larger unit (e.g. $1) until the costs have been added together. This process helps to minimize rounding error.
- Do as much as possible of the calculation and summarizing as you go along. In this way, you may be able to detect inconsistencies and odd results in time to check the information at its source.
- Note the source of each type of data as you collect it. A "source" note can be put at the bottom of a table or in some other place where it can be easily seen.

When you are doing cost calculations, your basic aim should be to identify all the inputs to the health care process and to quantify them in order to attach monetary values to them. In this module, we present basic ideas and methods for cost estimation and explain some additional steps that are generally recommended in order to obtain the real cost of a programme.

When you are making calculations, just as when you are collecting the data for them, try to distribute your efforts roughly in accordance with the relative importance of each cost category. For example, personnel costs are bound to be relatively large, so you should take particular care in their computation. For many programmes, less effort should be directed towards supplies and certain other categories identified below because of their relative unimportance to the total cost picture. The activities most needed for cost calculations will become clearer as each category of input is reviewed.

Capital (nonrecurrent) resource inputs

Capital goods are defined as inputs that last for more than one year. If you studied expenditure only in one particular year, you could easily get a distorted view of long-term average annual costs. For example, a great deal of equipment might have been purchased in the year *before* your study, with no expenditure on capital at all during the study period. One way to get an idea of long-term financial commitments is to:

- identify all the capital goods (vehicles, equipment, buildings, etc.) being used in that year;
- find out the current (replacement) cost of purchasing them (C);
- estimate the total number of years each is likely to last from when it was purchased (N) (the "working life" or "useful life");
- estimate the average annual cost of each capital item in terms of a simple "straight line" depreciation (C/N). A refinement of this approach favoured by economists is shown in Module 7.

Vehicles

The kinds of vehicles you may need to value include bicycles, motorcycles, four-wheel-drive vehicles, cars and trucks.

Costs to be included
Use the current cost for a similar vehicle, not the original purchase price. The cost should include freight.

Sources of cost data
Recent government contracts, supply records from donors, or local dealer estimates are useful sources of information.

Working life
The working life of a vehicle will vary considerably, depending on vehicle type, terrain, use and maintenance. Consequently, you should try to obtain a local consensus on the expected working life of each type of vehicle. Ask several people who use, drive or service cars for an estimate of how long this type of vehicle has lasted in the past (i.e. how long before the vehicle reached a stage where it was not worth repairing). For consistency, it is best to use the same time period (e.g. three or five years) for a given type of vehicle for the entire analysis, unless there are major differences in terrain, etc., that would justify the use of different figures.

In the unlikely event that some of the data described above are not available, a rough approximation to annual vehicle capital costs can be obtained from local rates for hiring vehicles. In such a case, the cost of vehicles looks like a recurrent, rather than a capital, item, but it should still be considered a capital cost.

Equipment

The kinds of equipment you may need to value include refrigerators, cold boxes, sterilizers, scales, insecticide sprayers and pumps. Use a reasonable figure for the cut-off point between supplies that last one year or more and genuine capital equipment—say, a unit price of $100.

Costs to be included

Use the current cost for a similar piece of equipment, not the original purchase price. The cost should include freight.

Sources of cost data

Recent government contracts, supply records from donors, or local dealer estimates are useful sources of information.

Working life

The working life of a piece of equipment can be ascertained by asking individuals who operate it how long this type of equipment generally lasts before it is beyond repair.

Buildings: space

The kinds of buildings you may need to value include health centres, hospitals, offices, staff houses and warehouses.

Costs to be included

You need to use the current cost of site development, architects' fees, construction costs and the cost of the land—i.e. how much it would cost to build the building *now*.

If the total cost is not available, you may be able to obtain estimates of the cost per unit area (e.g. per square metre) for the category of building you are interested in. You need to take into account factors that may influence those estimates, such as the distance from the capital city or the nature of the terrain, as well as the nature of the structure (e.g. building materials and number of storeys).

The cost of basic furnishings and built-in equipment should also be included. If it is impossible to itemize these separately, you could consider adding 10% to the total cost.

Sources of cost data

Recent government contracts for similar buildings are a useful source of information. The planning or tendering section of the health department, or architects in the Ministry of Works, or local construction firms should have this information. Quantity surveyors (if they exist in your country) can be helpful, too.

Working life

You should use 20 years as the expected working life of most buildings, unless they are very temporary structures with much shorter expected lives, or general past experience in your area clearly indicates a longer period.

The annual cost of building space can be estimated using an approach that will often be simpler to apply than the method described above. It consists of obtaining an estimate of the annual price charged for renting similar space. The estimate should distinguish between furnished and unfurnished buildings and between air-conditioned and non-air-conditioned space. In effect, this approach treats buildings as recurrent, instead of capital, inputs. (In that sense, it is similar to the approximation given earlier for vehicles.) You will probably need the assistance of a real-estate agent or someone else who is familiar with the rental market in your area.

In view of the relatively small value of building space in the total annual cost of a health programme, you will not need an accurate estimate for identical space. Even an approximation is likely to yield a cost estimate that is as accurate as one derived by applying the first, more complicated method (with its inevitable uncertainties regarding construction costs and years of useful life), especially for PHC programmes without hospitals.

Other capital inputs

For some programmes, at least at certain levels (usually the higher ones) of a health system, there will be relevant training and perhaps social mobilization activities. Some of these might be once-only, start-up activities, which constitute nonrecurrent (capital) inputs; others will be recurrent. In both cases, cost estimation is greatly simplified by adding up all the cost elements of a training or social mobilization programme (personnel, supplies, buildings, vehicles, etc.) and treating the cost as a lump sum.

If that cost total is for nonrecurrent activities (e.g. an initial staff training programme that will not be repeated), the same approach to annual costing should be used as for other capital items: divide the total cost by the estimated number of years of life (that is, the average number of years for which it affects the staff of your programme). For these categories of nonrecurrent inputs, as for others, the depreciation method of estimating annual costs can be modified to give more accurate economic estimates by the method described in Module 7.

Recurrent resource inputs

Personnel

Salaries, wages, and other expenses associated with personnel are frequently the single largest cost item in health programmes. You should therefore take great care in estimating their value. In most cases, you will be interested in both the staff directly involved in the activity you are concerned with (e.g. nurses, health aides, trainers, supervisors) and other support staff (e.g. managers, cleaners, guards, drivers). Naturally, you will only want to deal with the costs of the persons whose time, in whole or in part, is assigned to your programme (see "Allocating shared inputs", page 41).

Costs to be included

The full cost of employing someone is represented by the individual's gross earnings—that is, the take-home pay plus any additional benefits, such as contributions to health insurance, social security, and pension plans, and plus tax. These gross earnings should include any incentive payments, overtime, hardship bonuses, holiday and sick pay, and allowances for uniform, housing and travel. If the worker receives any additional commodities, housing or other nonmonetary benefits, the value of these should also be estimated, using the prevailing prices of similar items (e.g. the current market rent for similar housing).

Fees or honoraria for the short-term services of experts, advisers and others involved in the activity who are not employees should also be included.

Sources of cost data

Expenditure records and payrolls in the Ministry of Health will have cost data on salaries and allowances. You may need to look elsewhere for some data. For example, pensions may be paid by the Civil Service Board or another agency, and per diem allowances are often paid by external agencies. Data from the private market can help in the valuation of nonmonetary benefits, such as housing.

If you need to identify the earnings of particular individuals, ask for their salary grade rather than their actual salary. People are usually more reluctant to reveal their earnings than to state their position on a standard salary scale. Furthermore, it may be difficult to decide what the figure you are given means (gross or net salary, for example). Salary schedules can usually be obtained from the agency administering the civil service. Each type of information will need to be collected from the most appropriate level.

If you ask only about salary grades, you will not get information about other allowances and bonuses. A rough estimate could be made by assuming that the average ratio between salaries and allowances for the whole institution (or a relevant subgroup) can be applied to each individual. For example, you may find from district-level expenditure data that allowances are, on average, about 12% of salaries. You would then add an extra 12% to each individual's salary.

For practice in calculating personnel costs, see exercise 4A, page 116.

Supplies

This category is for materials used up in the course of the year, as direct inputs to the principal activities performed by the programme, and other small items purchased during the year. For example, for a disease control programme it could include such things as drugs, reagents for tests, insecticides for vector control, needles, slides and stationery. For an immunization programme, it would include vaccines, needles, syringes, cotton wool and surgical spirit, among other things. Although supplies will be a fairly big cost category for both the programmes mentioned, it will be relatively small for some other PHC activities and so will not justify a large effort. As already stated (page 33), you will need to establish a cut-off value that marks the boundary between supplies and equipment. For example, if the unit price of an item is less than $100 (or some other value that you set), even if it lasts for longer than one year, it will be simpler to consider it in the recurrent input category of supplies and count in full any such items purchased during the year. If the price of the item is $100 or higher, then the capital category—equipment—will be more appropriate. You might wish to distinguish between supplies acquired with local currency and supplies requiring foreign exchange. The general data handling process will be similar.

In some instances, it will be useful to identify separately, and summarize, major supply categories or categories of particular interest (i.e. calculate subtotals for drugs, stationery, vaccines, etc.).

Costs to be included
The full cost of supplies should include the cost of transport to the point of use (i.e. any freight charges for import of materials and any internal distribution costs). The cost should be that of all the material consumed, including any that is lost or wasted as well as that which is actually used for its intended purpose. Losses can result from misplaced shipments, damage (e.g. from water or rodents), pilfering and materials becoming out of date. This loss has to be paid for by the programme, and should be included in the estimates.

Supplies to be costed do *not* include those that are distributed but kept in store (as inventory stocks). Only those that are consumed should be counted.

Sources of cost data
Unless expenditure records are very detailed, they are unlikely to be useful for estimating the costs of most of the materials specific to your programme. Instead, you will need information on quantities and prices.

Quantities
For many supplies, there will be stores at different levels (national, regional, health centres), which will usually have their own inventory records. The quantity distributed from these stores during the year will be equal to the inventory at the beginning of the year *plus* the quantity received during the year *less* the inventory at the end of the year.

The amount distributed is not necessarily the amount consumed: commodities may be stored at a lower level. Only at the lowest level of the distribution system, such as the health centre, are supplies dispensed the same as supplies consumed. However, if you measure consumption only at the peripheral level, you will fail to take into account the wastage that has occurred between there and the point of original purchase.

You can calculate losses in the system by looking at each level and comparing "original stock + quantity received" with "final stock + quantity distributed". The difference reflects the amount lost at that level. This process can be refined by replacing "quantity distributed" by "quantity received by lower-level units"; the difference between these two values measures losses in transit between distribution points. This is a potentially complicated exercise, and it may be necessary to use rough approximations of the loss in the system; avoid spending too much time on this point.

Alternatively, if the flow of supplies is fairly steady, then the amount of supplies distributed from the higher-level unit may be a reasonably good approximation of the amount consumed at the peripheral units. This is a valid approximation only if peripheral units are not building up or running down stocks.

It is often possible to calculate the amount of supplies that should have been consumed on the basis of output. For example, if you know the number of children vaccinated against tuberculosis, you could calculate the amount of BCG vaccine that should have been used. This method is recommended only if data on wastage are readily available; as far as possible, local data should be used in preference to national averages.

Prices

Supply invoices, order forms, price lists and catalogues are sources of information about purchase prices or replacement prices. Costs of international and internal transport should be included. International freight costs can usually be readily determined (supply invoices and order forms should include them) and should not be overlooked, since they often add a further 10–20% to the original price. It may be more difficult to estimate internal transport costs; in fact, if supplies are transported by vehicles belonging to the programme, the costs will be included in the vehicle running costs and should not be included here.

Exercise 4B, page 117, contains questions to help you to apply some of the above observations on the cost of supplies.

Vehicles: operation and maintenance

Many health programmes rely on vehicles to distribute supplies, permit coordination and supervision, and otherwise implement the provision of care. All too often, transport is a weak link; vehicles are available but fail to operate efficiently because of a lack of fuel or spare parts. It is important to know what it costs to operate and maintain vehicles. Unfortunately, these costs are among the most difficult to measure. You will need to be persistent and imaginative in your efforts to collect such data. Fortunately, there are some ways of approximating the costs when the preferred sources are not helpful.

Costs to be included

The costs of operating, maintaining and repairing vehicles should all be measured. These will include materials, such as fuel, lubricants, insurance and registration fees, tyres, batteries and spare parts. The cost of drivers should be recorded under personnel. If a mechanic is assigned to the programme, the cost will also be included under personnel. However, where repairs and maintenance are contracted out, or where they are performed by a different office or agency, their cost should be included under vehicle operating costs (i.e. you should make an estimate of total repair costs, including an allowance for the mechanic's salary, rather than including the salary under personnel costs).

Sources of cost data

Expenditure records may give some indication of the cost of operating and maintaining vehicles, but it is likely that you will need to interview drivers and mechanics and consult logbooks to get a sufficiently detailed picture.

Fuel consumption is one input for which records are probably reasonably good. If not, you should be able to estimate fuel consumption based on the mileage of the vehicle. Logbooks should indicate distance travelled (say 5000 kilometres), and drivers should be able to tell you the average distance travelled per litre of fuel consumed for that particular type of car in the prevailing conditions (say 10 km per litre). Total consumption is then $5000/10 = 500$ litres. The price paid per litre for fuel multiplied by the number of litres used gives the total cost of the fuel (even if it is merely charged to a government account).

If logbooks and other information sources are not adequate for the calculations suggested (which is all too often the case), alternative data sources can probably be employed. For example, your ministry's central motor pool personnel may be able to give you a rough estimate of the total annual cost of operating and maintaining each type of vehicle. With information on the vehicles used (and the fraction of their time devoted to your programme) you can make a "rough and ready" calculation that will suffice.

Oil and filter changes and other maintenance may be done irregularly or on a routine basis, either after a set number of kilometres or at regular time intervals (e.g. once a year). If you are unable to calculate these inputs in the same way as fuel, you could simply increase fuel costs by a set percentage (e.g. 15%) to allow for them. Again, the central motor pool may help you with this.

Questions and answers concerning some aspects of operation and maintenance costs of vehicles can be found in exercise 4C, page 118.

Buildings: operation and maintenance

This category of inputs is quite easily handled. Although observers are some-times concerned with such costs as utility expenses, these do not form a large proportion of the total. If the approach below does not readily yield results (with little effort on your part), it should be replaced by a simple approximation: just draw on your past experience (and perhaps other expert opinions) to obtain a rough estimate for the total cost of building operation and maintenance as a proportion of their annual capital cost or the annual market rent for that amount of space. Multiply the annual capital cost recorded under "Buildings, space" by that percentage to obtain the desired recurrent cost value.

Costs to be included

Operation and maintenance costs for buildings should include charges for lighting, water, telephones, heating, insurance, cleaning materials, painting, and repairs to plumbing, roofing, heating and office furniture. As previously noted, the salaries of guards, cleaners, etc. should be counted under personnel.

Sources of cost data

This is one category where recorded expenditure data are sometimes quite adequate. Recurrent costs for buildings will normally be listed under such headings as "utilities", "maintenance" or "cleaning", and "security".

Training and social mobilization

On page 35, it was recommended that all the inputs to training and social mobilization programmes should be added together to give a single figure, rather than including them under separate headings (personnel, buildings, etc.). Each of these input categories has its recurrent counterpart, when activities are repeated periodically. The sum of these activities over one year is a recurrent cost of the programme.

There are probably no special problems involved, or instructions needed, for calculating the costs of these two categories of inputs. If a training or social mobilization programme serves more than one PHC programme, the total cost should be distributed among those served, as described on page 41.

Other operating inputs

This is, of course, the residual category, which covers all recurrent input costs not dealt with elsewhere. It will consist at most of a few relatively small cost elements not requiring great efforts of calculation. Most PHC programmes and their service delivery units, such as health centres, will not incur enough equipment-related recurrent costs to be worth identifying separately, but for the few exceptions you should use the following estimation method.

Costs to be included

Recurrent equipment costs include fuel (e.g. kerosene for cold-chain refrigerators) or electricity operating costs (but only if these are not included under buildings operation and maintenance), as well as the cost of spares for maintenance and repairs. Other categories might include postage, printing, photocopying and the costs of operating and maintaining equipment, but not stationery which is counted under supplies.

Sources of cost data

Expenditure records may contain some data, but they are unlikely to be detailed enough. For a piece of electrically operated equipment you will need to know its power requirements (the number of kilowatt-hours), the length of time it is operated over the year, and the cost per unit of electricity. You will probably need to ask the people directly responsible for the equipment about the kind of maintenance and repairs that were necessary and what spare parts were needed.

There are a variety of "rules of thumb" to estimate the likely operating and maintenance costs of equipment used in health programmes. Most of these rules relate recurrent costs to the original capital expenditure. The specific relationships will depend on the price structure in the country, the nature of the equipment, and so forth. You should explore the precise cost relationships in your own situation rather than relying on approximations from elsewhere.

Allocating shared inputs

If a particular input is used only for the PHC programme you are studying, then the entire cost of it can be assigned to that programme. However, often people, buildings, vehicles, social mobilization and supplies are used for many tasks, only some of which serve your programme. And within the programme there will be a variety of services that depend on shared inputs, such as the staff members who provide various types of care.

In some cases, the term "shared resources" simply means that the same types of input are used for different programmes or activities. For example, a particular type of drug may be used by two different disease control programmes. There may be practical difficulties in deciding how much of the drug was used for each, but there is no problem in theory. If your programme (and the underlying disease) did not exist, less of the drug would be required, and it is the value of this amount that represents the drug cost of the programme. You will need to examine the records showing the quantities of the drug used and the prices paid for it.

The situation is rather more difficult when a discrete input that cannot be split into smaller components (e.g. a person or vehicle) is shared. Depending on the kind of analysis you wish to do, it may not always be necessary to measure inputs that are shared with other programmes. Suppose, for example, that you wanted to know the finances required for the first few years of a programme. The programme may be so small that it can be accommodated in existing buildings and use existing vehicles. Since these resources would be paid for even if the new programme were not implemented, it would not be appropriate to include them in estimates of the additional finance required. In that respect, there is no incremental cost of buildings and vehicles for the *new* programme.

Unfortunately, this rarely happens. It is often difficult to relate general health administration and management, for instance, to separate programmes. This does not mean that additional programmes can be taken on without increasing management and administrative capacities. Unless a new programme is very small, any extra capacity (e.g. spare time or space) that might have existed in the health system will quickly be used up and additional resources will be required. Thus, any new scheme is likely to involve incremental costs.

You therefore need to find a reasonably accurate way of dividing the costs of shared resources among various user programmes. This process is called *cost allocation*. Its importance—and difficulty—will vary among programmes and levels of service.

It is helpful to start by thinking about the particular components of the various inputs that determine costs. The table below lists for each type of resource the component that most directly determines the cost.

Input	Component that determines cost
Vehicles	Distance travelled/time used
Equipment	Time used
Building space	Time used/space used
Personnel	Time worked
Supplies	Weight/volume
Vehicle operation and maintenance	Distance travelled/time used
Building operation and maintenance	Time used/space used
Other inputs	Miscellaneous

Ideally you should use these components directly as the basis for allocating costs. So, for personnel, you should measure the time that they devote to your programme; for a shared vehicle, you should measure the distance travelled or the time used for duties related to your programme. Similar approaches apply to other categories of shared resources. In some cases, this is relatively straight-forward: for example, staff may have specific periods of the day or week which they devote to the immunization programme, or particular rooms in a building may be used for immunization. In other cases, allocation is less simple.

It is especially important to get an accurate measure of the proportion of time that staff members spend on the activities you are interested in. The reason for this, apart from the basic importance of personnel costs, is that this proportion is often used to allocate other shared costs. For example, if you cannot measure the proportion of vehicle costs that should be allocated to the immunization programme, you can use the proportion of staff time devoted to the programme as a way of allocating the value of shared vehicle costs. If half the staff time during a particular session is devoted to immunization, it is reasonable to assume that half the transport is, too.

In many cases, it is not easy to measure staff time. Immunization, for instance, may be done as part of general well-baby clinics, with staff in any one session handling a number of different activities. There are some highly accurate, but not necessarily practicable, ways of measuring time. For example, because it is risky to rely on staff members' memories of how they distributed their time when you interview them later, you can:

- Arrange for staff to fill out time sheets routinely or over a certain period of time (this procedure requires supervision to be reliable);
- Directly observe staff on a random sample of days, recording what they do every half-hour. This procedure entails considerable expense and effort, and is rarely feasible.

The above procedures are often impractical, so it is necessary, instead, to use proxies—variables that you expect to be closely related to the direct determinants of cost. A useful proxy for allocating personnel costs is the proportion of visits or contacts that are made for a particular function. For example, you could assume that the proportion of time spent by staff on treating acute respiratory infections is the same as the proportion of health centre visits made for such infections. The assumption is that time and visits increase in the same way. To estimate the recurrent costs of vehicles used for a maternal and child health programme in the absence of records of distance travelled, you could look at the time the vehicle is used for your activity, assuming that each trip is for a designated programme. The assumption is that time and distance are closely related.

If you are not measuring the factor that directly determines costs, but are relying on a proxy, you should be aware of the assumptions that underlie your choice of proxy. If these assumptions are not true, the proxy may not be accurate. For example, allocating salaries according to the proportion of visits for acute respiratory infections assumes that a visit for such an infection requires the same amount of time as a visit for other illnesses and takes no account of a patient with more than one complaint. If there is no reasonable proxy and none of the more accurate methods is feasible, you might have to make some kind of direct measurement. Usually, though, you can find some way of achieving your aims with a reasonable margin of error without resorting to that. Assuming that the necessary information is available, exercise 4D, page 119, provides an illustration of allocations.

MODULE 5
Measuring effectiveness

In previous modules, some of the uses to which cost information can be put were identified. One of the applications mentioned was *efficiency*. This takes into account the benefits of an activity as well as its costs, and weighs up the "pros" and "cons".

Many different terms are used to describe the "other side of the coin" of an activity or programme. We may refer to consequences, outcomes, outputs, benefits, results, impact or effects. These terms are similar, but they cannot all be used interchangeably. A major distinction in economic language is between "benefits" which, strictly speaking, refer only to outcomes that can be measured in terms of money, and "effectiveness" or "effects", which are outcomes that are not expressed in financial terms, such as the number of lives saved by a health intervention.

Because of the difficulty of defining all the important outcomes of health programmes in money terms (how do you value life?), this manual focuses on effectiveness rather than benefits. Effectiveness is a measure of the extent to which objectives are achieved. Most PHC programmes have as their ultimate objective an improvement in the health status of the populations they serve, e.g. a reduced incidence of immunizable diseases or an improvement in the health of mothers and children.

Module 9 shows how costs and effectiveness can be combined to derive a measure of efficiency; this is cost-effectiveness analysis. For now, it is sufficient for you to think about efficiency in terms of cost divided by effectiveness, such as the cost per life saved by a programme:

$$\frac{\text{cost}}{\text{number of lives saved}}$$

Choosing an indicator of effectiveness

There are a number of indicators or measures of effectiveness that reflect *intermediate* changes rather than final outcomes. For example, before a nutrition education programme can be successful in reducing malnutrition and mortality, the educational message must reach the communities; these communities must then respond by changing the type of foods they eat or the way they prepare food. These intermediate outcomes, such as the number of people exposed to the message or the number changing their behaviour, can serve as partial measures of effectiveness. Their chief advantage is the relative ease with which they can be measured and interpreted. Even when the final health status data are not available, these intermediate measures can usually give some indication of the results.

To give an example based on an oral rehydration programme: the use of inputs (e.g. staff and oral rehydration salts (ORS)) indicates the provision of services (e.g. delivery of ORS packets and guidance on how and why to use them) that have intermediate effects (e.g. improved knowledge and attitudes causing mothers to use ORS for their children), which in turn produce long-term effects on health status (e.g. a decline in mortality among children under five).

Without doing a full-scale exercise now, take a few minutes to list for yourself the answers to the following key questions about the effects of your health programme:

- What are the main objectives of your programme?
- Which of these objectives, or which combination of them, can be expressed in terms of a single indicator of health status?
- What are three important intermediate outputs of your programme?

When you do a cost-effectiveness analysis, you will be comparing at least two things—for instance, two ways of organizing your programme or activity, or two different sets of inputs to your programme. Ideally, you should choose a measure of effectiveness that captures all the important differences between the alternatives that you are comparing. For example, say you are comparing two different messages used in the mass media to promote contraceptive use. The number of people exposed to each message is *not* a satisfactory outcome measure to use in this case, since merely hearing a message does not guarantee that the hearer will change behaviour and the different messages are likely to have different effects on contraceptive use. You would really need to measure changes in the rate of contraceptive use.

On the other hand, if one alternative was to broadcast a given message at six o'clock in the evening and the other was to broadcast the same message at eight o'clock in the evening, the number of people in the target group exposed to the message is quite an appropriate measure. If you were comparing two completely different contraceptive methods, then neither the numbers exposed to the message nor the use of contraceptives would be adequate: it would be necessary to use a measure of impact, such as months of effective birth control or even the birth rate (though the latter will be affected only over a long period of time).

Usually, the greater the difference in the alternatives you are comparing, the more likely it is that you will need a measure of changes in health status, rather than changes in the output of goods and services, if you want to compare their outcomes.

At the same time, you should be aware that the further you move away from immediate outputs and the closer you get to health impact, the harder it will be to make the measurements. Measuring changes in health status is a difficult and expensive task. It often involves establishing baseline surveys and follow-up surveys, collecting data on a number of variables, and surveying large populations. Even if you do successfully measure a change, it is likely to be quite difficult to demonstrate what caused it and, in particular, how much of the change was due to the intervention you are interested in. Measures of effects on behaviour or knowledge pose similar, though perhaps less severe, difficulties.

For these reasons, it is recommended that you focus on *service* outputs as your effectiveness measures (e.g. number of children immunized, number of contraceptives distributed, number of treatments provided). These data are often collected routinely and are usually available in existing records. Then, where possible, you can move on to examine effects on health status.

Comparisons involving more than one measure of effectiveness are considerably more difficult to interpret. However, sometimes it is difficult to identify (or to measure) a single outcome variable that satisfactorily embodies all the differences between the options you are considering. In this case, you could choose more than one. For example, say you were comparing two different staffing structures for your health facilities; you might decide that you want to know how these compare in terms of number of immunizations, prenatal sessions and home visits.

For practice in dealing with some of the issues discussed above, see exercise 5A, page 122.

Judging the merits of measures of effectiveness

There are many things to consider in assessing the merits or adequacy of any potential measure of effectiveness. Several important considerations are presented below.

Is the effectiveness measure comparable between alternatives?

Ideally, you need to choose an outcome measure that means the same thing for all the interventions you are comparing. In other words, you want an outcome measure whose numerical value will reflect the difference between the alternatives. It is not very helpful to use an outcome measure which is different in *quality* for the alternatives you are examining, particularly if these have different implications for health impact.

For example, the outcome "number of births attended" could have very different implications for health impact if one option involves doctors in a hospital setting and the other traditional birth attendants in a village. A preliminary assessment of relative knowledge and skills from a sample of the two groups would give you some clues to decide whether the consequences for health are likely to be similar. These data on quality will indicate whether the link between the intermediate outcome you have chosen and the health impact is likely to be the same for each of the options. If there is little difference in quality, then there is no problem with using "number of births attended". If the differences appear to be significant, you could:

- choose an outcome measure closer to the health impact end of the spectrum (e.g. perinatal mortality);

  or

- redefine your outcome measure so that it includes some of the quality dimensions, for example: "births attended by trained personnel and in which the umbilical cord is handled under sterile conditions" or "institutional births".

To consider another example, assume that you are studying prenatal programmes in two districts that aim to serve the same number of women, and you find that both districts have weekly prenatal classes attended by about 50 women. Does this mean that the prenatal parts of both MCH programmes are equally effective in ensuring the health of mothers? In what ways might they differ? You might consider looking into at least four factors:

- the number of prenatal visits;
- the number of tetanus toxoid injections given to the women;
- whether the women are correctly assessed for their "at risk" status (using such criteria as age, height, family size, pregnancy history, nutritional status and chronic disease);
- whether appropriate decisions on treatment or referral are made on the basis of the risk assessment.

You could assess the similarity of the two districts with respect to these factors. If you suspect that the districts are rather different, you might devise a new measure that incorporates those quality dimensions, such as "the number of women who make at least two prenatal visits, are assessed for risk and appropriately treated and referred, and receive two tetanus toxoid injections".

Because the quality of treatment is important, you should consider using effectiveness measures that specify a certain quality of output, such as "patients treated effectively".

You should also check whether the patients are comparable. Are their health problems similar in seriousness? Is the case mix similar?

If you are considering the numbers treated for a certain condition, there are four other major factors that you ought to take into account when thinking about ways in which effectiveness indicators may differ in their implications for health. These factors, together with the numbers covered (by treatment, prevention, education, etc.), determine health impact. They are:

- compliance of patients with treatment prescribed;
- diagnostic accuracy;
- compliance of physicians with established protocols;
- efficiency, i.e. effectiveness in relation to cost.

Naturally, you might be limited in dealing with these factors by lack of time or other obstacles. You can do only as much as is practicable.

Does the measure of effectiveness have side-effects?

A second aspect of all measures of effectiveness that you should consider is their *comprehensiveness.* The step-by-step process mentioned above, in which basic inputs are transformed into health impacts via intermediate outcomes, is clearly a simplification. There are likely to be offshoots from this main path. It is easy to neglect these, particularly if they are unintentional or negative in their effects (e.g. the occasional adverse side-effects of vaccination). If you suspect that the frequency of these other outcomes is different for the alternatives you are considering, you should note them, at least, and measure them if possible.

For example, you may be comparing two different vaccines against cholera. You find that they are equally effective in reducing the incidence of cholera. However, one vaccine has occasional side-effects. These effects should be reported as part of your comparative analysis. Your results can then be used to decide to what extent the side-effects should influence policy.

Another illustration of possible side-effects can be found in exercise 5B, page 123.

Does the measure cover the most desirable effect?

The indicators of effectiveness should reflect the outcome in which you are most interested: the intervention with the greatest effectiveness is the best (though it might also be more expensive and less efficient). The desirable outcomes may seem obvious: more staff trained, more drugs distributed, less malnutrition, and so forth. But you need to think carefully about the programme's ultimate goal and whether your measure reflects it.

For example, a reduction in malnutrition may appear to be an unquestionable objective of a nutrition programme. However, a successful nutrition programme may actually lead to an *increase* in the number of malnourished children because it saves some children who would otherwise have died, but who remain malnourished. You must decide what you want to achieve so that you can pick the best measure. (Here, a combined mortality/malnutrition indicator might be appropriate.)

Is the measure sufficiently sensitive?

Deaths in children under five years of age may seem like a good indicator (though difficult to measure) of the effectiveness of a diarrhoeal diseases control programme. In fact, however, it may actually obscure the achievements of the programme by being too stringent. Even when deaths from diarrhoea are reduced, overall child mortality may remain the same. This seems to be because children saved from death from diarrhoea are often weak and are likely to die anyway from other causes, notably measles.

If reducing child mortality is the ultimate goal, then the programme would be judged unsuccessful in a sample analysis. Yet some would argue that the reduction in diarrhoea deaths has a value in itself. It does, after all, represent some increase in life expectancy, and can be seen as a prerequisite for other disease control measures to have an impact on overall child mortality.

Alternative measures of effectiveness in this case are not easily found, but there is a need for them. One might be the average number of years survived after treatment (if measurable). What would you suggest?

Measuring effectiveness

One way to estimate effectiveness is to measure the change in an indicator over the period you are interested in. This is valid only if you have reason to believe that the change is a result of the resource inputs to your programme. The procedure for this estimation is sketched out here. It is kept brief because of the assumption that underlies this manual, namely, that you already have some experience of designing or interpreting evaluation studies, and know about control or comparison groups and other relevant points. If you do not know enough about these things, you can supplement this module by further reading or by talking with a specialist in evaluation.

To measure change in an indicator of effectiveness you need to know its value before and after the measurement period. Sometimes this is easy: for example, the number of staff trained in a training programme can readily be found (though their subsequent deployment might not be so easy to follow). Sometimes it is very difficult. To find out whether there are fewer deaths in a community, and whether the lower death rate is attributable to your programme, may be quite difficult; you need to know how many deaths there were before the programme started and how many afterwards. If these statistics are not collected routinely, you may have to do community surveys.

If you cannot collect data on all events (that is, all the deaths in the community), you will need to take a sample. The sample should be large enough to enable you to detect any important changes. Often sampling requires some technical assistance.

You will need to decide how much of the change that you observe is due to the intervention you are interested in. Sometimes this is easy. For example, if your measure of the effectiveness of a nutrition education programme is the number of mothers attending classes, you can monitor this directly. However, if the indicator you choose is the reduction in malnutrition, it may be quite difficult to work out whether the changes in malnutrition were due to the education programme or some other factor, such as a good harvest.

In such cases, where it is difficult to trace effectiveness, it may be necessary to compare your test group with a population that was *not* exposed to the intervention (i.e. where there was no nutrition education programme). Ideally all other features of the second group should be the same. This should tell you whether the change would have happened even without the intervention. These comparison groups are called "controls".

Some effectiveness measures can be derived from others. For example, it is possible to measure the effectiveness of a vaccination programme in controlling disease incidence either directly, or by the following approach:

$$effectiveness = number\ vaccinated \times efficacy\ of\ the\ vaccine.$$

However, this assumes that you already know the efficacy of the vaccine.

Many health-related outcomes, and some service inputs and effects, vary throughout the year. It is therefore important to measure these effects over the whole year. It will probably be difficult to measure all the effects; for example, health facilities may not collate their data into annual figures or monthly statistics and may not report them promptly. You may therefore need to take a sample, using a random selection of daily or weekly records (see the discussion of sampling in Module 3).

In some cases, the effects of a programme will continue beyond the period of the investment. For example, an education programme may affect behaviour in the long term. If you are able to measure these long-term effects, you will need to adjust them in order to include them in the measurement of the effectiveness of your programme. Technical assistance will probably be needed for this "discounting" step (which is covered in more detail in Module 10).

Locating data on effectiveness

In the interests of practical assessment of programmes, you would do well to concentrate on identifying suitable measures of effectiveness that can be obtained from existing records. If the data currently being collected routinely are really inadequate for your purposes, investigate the possibility of improving the system within the limits of your time and resources. Some of the common sources of routinely collected data are listed below, together with an indication of the types of data that may be useful as measures of effectiveness. Where it is not obvious in the table, you may find it useful to identify the specific types of programme to which each measure could be applied.

You should be alert to the possibility of using other surveys or censuses to collect your effectiveness data. If a study of behavioural changes or health impact is being conducted for other reasons, you should take the opportunity to incorporate a cost analysis into it, provided that its staff can accommodate your needs.

Source of data	Type of data
Health facility data (clinic registers, patient records)	Attendance at preventive and curative sessions; diagnosis; laboratory results; treatment, drugs, and contraceptives prescribed and distributed; nutrition status
Hospital data	As above and, for inpatients, the outcome of treatment; data on previous treatment; number of births in the hospital
Campaign reports	Vaccinations given in immunization campaigns; no. of people starting to use contraception as a result of family planning campaigns
Laboratory records	Diagnosis of certain conditions (e.g. malaria, cholera)
Notifiable diseases registers	Incidence of notifiable diseases
Inventories	Amount of drugs produced, delivered or distributed
Infant mortality	Major causes of death
TBA and community records	Low birth weight

Expressing measures of effectiveness

Your measure of effectiveness has to be quantitative. It could be in figures, such as 50 children vaccinated, or 30 000 capsules produced, or 1200 visits. It is also possible to express effectiveness as a proportion, for example the percentage of children vaccinated. Proportions are a useful measure of coverage, but can be difficult to interpret in combination with cost data. We do not recommend that you use them. Express your results as a single number rather than a ratio whenever possible. An example of this would be the *number* of children who have been immunized, rather than the *proportion* of the target population.

You should define as precisely as possible what your effectiveness indicator means. If the effects are expressed in terms of people, you should consider whether it is necessary to define age, sex and place of residence. You should also specify as precisely as possible the event you are measuring. If your outcome is "number of people treated for disease X", be precise about the kind of treatment that you are including and about your definition of the disease as well as the group of people. If your outcome is "number of staff to do task Y", give precise details of the task and the staff members who are to be included. If your outcome is "amount of service Z produced", define Z as precisely as you can. In this way, you are forced to be entirely clear about what you are measuring, and the remainder of the analysis will be much easier.

Now complete this module by doing exercises 5C and 5D, pages 123–125.

MODULE 6

Calculating unit financial costs

It is now time to put together some of the key ideas and measures that you have already studied, especially those concerning health service costs (Module 4) and effects (Module 5). They are used here to calculate unit costs. This module is a short one, setting the stage for the refinements and extensions to come in part B and the applications described in part C.

General nature of unit costs

A unit cost is a kind of simple average—the cost per unit of output or outcome. It can be applied to many things in the analysis of PHC, as illustrated in the next section.

The basic calculation of a unit cost (often called average cost) is not difficult. Where the total cost and the quantity of output have been found:

$$\text{unit cost} = \frac{\text{total cost}}{\text{quantity}}$$

It is important to remember that at this point we are concerned with unit *financial* costs, i.e. costs expressed in terms of financial outlay. Other types of unit costs, in which cost is defined to include other economic dimensions, are considered in later modules.

Examples of unit costs

By the time you have finished this manual, you will have calculated and put to use many kinds of unit costs. For now, though, it is helpful to see what measures have been used in one kind of PHC programme, namely an immunization programme. Some important unit cost measures for immunizations—by no means all—are given below:

- for an immediate service (output): cost per dose administered (this could be subdivided by type of vaccine);
- for an intermediate effect: cost per fully immunized child (this could be subdivided by vaccine);
- for a final effect or impact on health status: cost per case averted or per death averted (elaborations might include cost per year of life saved).

These examples of unit costs are based on the assumption that the appropriate costs can be assigned or allocated to each output or outcome involved. For example, if the immunization programme is part of a wider maternal and child health (MCH) effort, its cost must be separated from other MCH costs. For antigen-specific measures within the programme, all relevant costs must be estimated; for example, to calculate the cost per dose of measles vaccine administered, only the portion of total costs reasonably attributable to measles vaccination (vaccine plus a proportion of all shared costs) should be used.

Naturally, illustrations of unit costs can be found at all levels of the health system. The manager of a health centre will be concerned with the unit cost of services. A regional programme director might wish to compare cost per dose for all health centres and other service delivery sites within a district or region, while the national immunization programme director will be interested in average values for all the regions of the country. An MCH programme director will wish to know the costs of a variety of primary services, not just immunizations, and probably site by site.

For some initial practice in organizing information, in preparation for calculating and interpreting the unit costs of a different kind of health programme (malaria control), see exercise 6A, page 126.

Uses of unit costs

Calculating unit financial costs is straightforward in principle, but the practical results will only be as good as the elements that go into each calculation. If your estimates of total cost or quantity are flawed, your unit costs will be, too.

The uses of cost analysis will frequently justify your efforts in working through this manual and putting what you have learned to use in real studies of your own. Some of the uses of cost analysis have been described in earlier modules, and others will be dealt with later. Certain of them rely on simple unit costs of outputs, which allow you to compare the administrative efficiency of various service delivery units. Others involve intermediate effects as the denominators for preliminary cost-effectiveness analysis; the example we used earlier was cost per fully immunized child. More ambitious cost-effectiveness analyses are directed at health status impacts, using, for example, a measure of cost per death averted.

You will also find it useful to break down the cost estimates by type of input. It is especially useful to be able to isolate personnel costs and examine them over time or across delivery units to see how efficiently staff are being used. That application and others are discussed further in later modules.

Cost-effectiveness analysis

MODULE 7

Measuring and using economic costs

What are economic costs?

Costs are often thought of in terms of money paid for resources used; but there is a broader way of looking at costs that can be useful in some cases. The basic idea is that things have a *value* that might not be fully captured in their *price*. It is not difficult in many health programmes to identify resource inputs for which little or no money is paid: volunteers working without payment; health messages broadcast without charge; vaccines or other supplies donated or provided at a large discount by organizations or individuals.

Should we say that these inputs cost nothing? The answer depends on what you are interested in. For some purposes, there is no need to take into account resources that are not paid for. This is true, for example, if your concern is solely to determine how much of a financial budget allocation was actually spent. Resources for which you paid nothing do not appear as expenditure and can be ignored (i.e. their financial cost is zero).

However, if you are concerned with the long-term sustainability of your programme, the total cost of all inputs—even those temporarily provided by donors or paid for at below market rates—must be estimated. In addition, public officials should be concerned with the full resource consequences of implementing a health programme. In marshalling resources for the benefit of one programme, society is forfeiting the opportunity to use them for some alternative activity. This lost opportunity is a cost that society bears. For example, the time that volunteers devote to your health programme might be time that they would otherwise use to work on their land or in a paid job. The return they would get from these alternative activities is a measure of the cost of the time they devote to your programme.

Economists use the terms "opportunity cost" or "economic cost" to describe this approach to costing. It recognizes the cost of using resources that could have been productively used elsewhere.

Analyses using economic costs do not replace those using financial costs, but supplement them with additional information useful for decision-making.

How to measure economic costs

Donated goods and services

The types of goods and services commonly donated to health programmes by individuals and communities include labour, construction materials and food.

Private and public enterprises frequently provide resources, such as free time on television or radio, newspaper space and transport. The easiest way to value donated goods and services is to look at the prices they command in the open market. For example, in the case of radio time you could find out what the radio station normally charges for advertising (if this is what it would otherwise do with the time slot allocated to your programme), taking into account the duration and time of day. For volunteer labour, you could find out whether those people receive a salary or wages elsewhere and use that to cost their donated time. If they are not currently employed, you could use wage rates paid to workers who do equivalent work in the health system, or the average agricultural wage in the area, or the current minimum wage.

When you make allowances for donations or any other adjustments of the kinds covered in this module in order to estimate economic costs, be sure to label your cost results clearly, stating which costs are economic ones and which are financial ones. To consider donated resources further, as part of economic cost estimation, see exercise 7A, page 127.

Other inputs whose price is incorrect

The concept of opportunity or economic cost has applications beyond valuing non-paid-for resources. It also calls into question the appropriateness of the prices used in valuing *all* resources, even those that are paid for. It cannot be assumed that the price paid for the resources used in your programme always reflects the true value of those resources to society. Economists use the term "shadow price" to refer to a price that has been adjusted for various reasons, including donations, to yield economic cost.

Shadow pricing may be needed in other situations where an input price is incorrect (in an economic sense), for example, where a resource used in a programme has been subsidized so that it appears to be worth less than it really is. An illustration might be a medical specialist who is paid partly by the programme and partly from some other national source of funds or even by an external aid organization. Someone is paying the subsidy that enables your programme to receive the resource relatively cheaply. Similarly, with inputs that are taxed, your department or programme may be paying extra, but those extra funds are simply transferred and used for other purchases, and should not be included in estimating the economic costs of that resource.

Costing is never complete or perfect when you have to deal with prices that have been distorted by taxes, subsidies or other factors. Where a distortion appears to have an appreciable effect on total costs—personnel is a good example—you should attempt to present the results both with and without appropriate adjustment. For example, legislation may fix minimum or maximum prices for some resources: a minimum wage for workers is a common example. Setting a minimum wage artificially increases the price of lower-level labour. In other words, some people are being paid at a rate that does not reflect the value of their output. The cost to society of employing them in the programme is not represented accurately by their wage, but by some lesser amount that reflects the value of their output in employment where there is no minimum wage. In situations of high unemployment, the economic cost of labour may be close to zero—another potentially important case.

Inputs that require foreign exchange pose other complications for calculating true costs. Important equipment and supplies, such as certain drugs, are often imported and thus require foreign exchange. If you want to value them in economic-cost terms, you must use an exchange rate to express the value of the foreign currency in terms of domestic currency. The exchange rate set by government may be unrealistic in comparison with actual currency market rates. Usually, foreign exchange is in short supply in developing countries. However, the official exchange rate often does not reflect this fact and makes foreign exchange appear to be cheaper than it really is, thus undervaluing imported inputs. Health officials generally cannot be expected to make exchange rate adjustments, but help should be available, especially for higher-level (e.g. national) cost analyses. If you are involved in such studies, seek advice from the government planning office, the Ministry of Finance or the central bank about the appropriate "shadow prices" to use for foreign exchange as well as labour.

Capital inputs

The special nature of capital (nonrecurrent) inputs and methods of estimating their financial costs on an annual-equivalent or other basis were described in Module 4. With economic costs, you will usually be concerned with the cost of resources used over a specific period (say, one year), rather than at the time they are purchased. For recurrent costs, resources purchased and resources used in a given year are likely to be very similar. Differences will only exist if the programme is not in equilibrium, and stocks are being either built up or run down. However, capital items are, by their nature, bought in one year and used for several years more. As explained in Module 4, we need a way of spreading out the costs over the study period. Module 4 shows one approach which is valid for most purposes: simply divide the total capital cost by the number of years of the item's expected life to give a kind of depreciation. However, this is not adequate if you are interested in economic costs, which must take into account the value of alternative opportunities for using the resources tied up in the capital inputs.

We present below an approach to economic costing of capital. This approach has some disadvantages and is not always used in health cost studies. It is not as simple as depreciation, which discourages some potential users, especially at the local level. In addition, its basic concern for alternative uses of resources ignores the fact that the costs of tying up funds might be of greater importance to other agencies than to the Ministry of Health or a particular programme (or, to put it differently, that certain capital costs do not accrue to the ministry or programme). Still, estimates of the economic cost of capital inputs can provide useful information, especially from the perspective of national allocation of scarce resources, so it is worth considering a reasonable way of making them. The approach is described here for the case of equipment, but it could also apply to vehicles. Costing of another important category of nonrecurrent inputs, building space, is probably better achieved by estimates based on the rental value, as explained in Module 4. That module also suggested a cut-off value of $100 to distinguish equipment from supplies.

Consider the example of a piece of equipment which costs $10 000 and has a useful life of 10 years. To suggest that this is equivalent to $1000 per year (10 000/10) is to overlook a very important fact. If you invest the $10 000 in this piece of equipment, that money will be tied up for the whole period of 10 years. On the other hand, if you are only paying out $1000 per year, you could be reinvesting the rest ($9000 in the first year) and earning interest. After 10 years of paying out $1000 a year, you would have some money left over from your accumulated interest. In other words, a $10 000 initial payment actually means paying out *more* than $1000 per year. The precise amount depends on the earnings the money would otherwise have made (i.e. the interest rate). Fortunately, there are tables which make the necessary calculations quite straightforward.

To calculate the economic cost of equipment on an "annualized" (cost per year) basis, use the following approach.

- *Current value.* Estimate the current value of the capital item, as the amount you would have to pay to purchase a similar item now (i.e. the replacement value rather than the original price).
- *Useful life.* Estimate the total number of years of useful life the item can realistically be expected to have (from the time of purchase).
- *Discount rate.* Find out the discount rate used by the economic planning office or Ministry of Finance. (A more difficult approach would be to calculate the real rate of interest, i.e. the rate of interest that could be obtained by depositing money in the bank minus the rate of inflation, while a simpler approach would be to accept a "high side" World Bank discount rate of 10%.)
- *Annualization factor.* Consult a standard table (page 142) to find the correct annualization factor.
- *Calculation of annual cost.* Calculate the annual cost by dividing the current value of the item by the annualization factor.

For a single $10 000 piece of equipment, the approach above would be applied as follows:

- *Current value*: $10 000
- *Useful life*: 5 years

- *Discount rate*: 10%
- *Annualizing factor (from standard table)*: 3.791
- *Calculation of annual economic cost*: $10 000/3.791 = $2638 per year (rounded figure).

To compare this *economic* cost with the corresponding *financial* cost, note that the latter would be $10 000/5 = $2000 per year. The investment of funds "up front" to pay for the equipment in full at the start of its use raises the annual cost—which is to be expected. See exercise 7B, page 127, for practice in such calculations.

Summary

In many situations, economic costs and financial costs are equivalent. Use financial costs as a starting-point for estimating economic costs; then check the following three features and make adjustments if necessary:

- *Donated goods or services.* These should be valued and included in economic costs.
- *Distorted prices.* Check with the planning office whether salaries and the official exchange rate are valid measures of the value of labour and foreign exchange, respectively.
- *Capital.* Instead of using expenditure and depreciation, calculate the annualized value of capital items being employed, using an appropriate discount rate.

How to use economic costs

As already discussed, economic costs can be thought of as a measure of the total cost to society of providing a health programme. But this really serves as a description of what economic costs are, rather than as an explanation of their usefulness. To complete this module, we outline below some practical applications of economic costs. Some aspects of this outline will be further elaborated in Part C.

One important reason for collecting data on the cost of resources used in your programme is that you can better predict what the future budgetary demands are likely to be. Donated goods and services do not place demands on the current budget, but it is unrealistic to expect that donors, whether external or local, will always be prepared to support the programme. What would happen if the current sources of donated goods or voluntary labour dried up? It is useful to have a rough idea of how much money would be required if contributions of a particular resource were to decline, or cease entirely.

A second reason for measuring the cost of donated resources is that this can provide a useful indicator of the capacity of government resources to generate contributions from the community or other sources. At the same time, it gives some idea of the popular appeal of different programmes, indicating areas where donations might be increased.

The most important reason for calculating costs, which is explored in more detail in Module 9, is to measure the relative efficiency of different ways of implementing a programme. This involves assessing what has to be sacrificed in order to achieve a specified goal. The government could take a limited perspective and decide to look at ways of maximizing the effectiveness of its own financial resources. But adopting a limited perspective often does not make sense for government bodies. They should usually be concerned with society as a whole. In other words, they should take into account *all* the resources employed and not just the ones they pay for. And the answers you get can be very different, depending on your definition of costs. The broader perspective is especially important for administrators and policy-makers at the highest level.

Consider, for example, the manager of a water supply project whose budget covers the purchase of pumps but not their installation, which is the responsibility of the community. She has the choice of two pumps. They both work equally well, but one is slightly cheaper and requires much more labour to install. If the manager were concerned simply with maximizing the returns of the financial investment, she would probably purchase the cheaper pumps, since she can get more of them for the same money. In doing so, however, she is probably placing a substantial burden on individuals, especially those at lower levels of the health system, who will have to do more installation work. The sacrifice they are called on to make may be so substantial that the pumps are not, in fact, installed, thereby rendering the initial investment worthless. If the manager had taken into account the community resources required, she might well have chosen the slightly more expensive pumps. Thus, it would be desirable to take a broad view of pump selection, based on *economic* costs. (Of course, there are other costs to consider in this case—for example, the cost of maintaining the pumps after installation.)

Economic costs can also be used in the same way as financial costs. Calculating annualized economic costs encourages you to think about: cost per unit of service as an indicator of efficiency; cost per beneficiary, per head, or per household as a measure of equity; and cost per head as a measure of priority. It is only when it comes to certain aspects of affordability and to comparisons with budget allocations that it is inappropriate to use economic costs rather than financial costs.

To conclude your review of the economic costs of a programme, you will find it useful—even necessary—to prepare a summary table of economic costs of each standard category of inputs, identifying the source that has provided or supported the cost. Then you can calculate the full programme costs. This process is partly illustrated in exercise 7C, page 128.

MODULE 8

Household costs

In Module 7, we explained about costs that embrace more than simply the amount paid for resources. You were encouraged to consider the complete economic costs borne by society in providing the services of your programme. Here, the concept of costs is extended to those incurred by people receiving health care—the consumers. This goes a long way beyond costs confined to producers. You might wish to consider household costs for special purposes, including setting fees when cost recovery is an objective. At other times— probably for most studies—you will not have to go so far in your collection and interpretation of cost data. Nevertheless, you should know something about household costs to broaden your range of skills in cost analysis.

What are household costs?

From the perspective of society as a whole, the costs of obtaining health care and other services are just as pertinent as the costs of producing services. Economists would say that the "demand" side of health service utilization is as pertinent as the "supply" side.

What are the principal elements of the costs incurred in receiving care? To take advantage of the treatment or education available in a health centre, people need to travel to the centre and wait their turn. To do this, they may have to take time off from paid work and forfeit wages. Or they may sacrifice useful time at home. They may have to pay for public transport, consultations and medicines. If houses are sprayed with insecticide for malaria control, householders may need to vacate their premises and empty their houses of goods. To receive health education through radio broadcasts, people may need to purchase batteries and spend time listening to the programmes.

Costs in *time* are especially important. A study of treatment for malaria in Thailand found that about 90% of estimated costs to patients were time costs. You can probably provide information about this from your own experience. Not only the patients but also other members of the household are likely to be involved, spending time caring for patients or accompanying them to the place where health care is delivered. Costs may also be incurred by people who go to health facilities but receive no treatment. They may find that the health centre is closed, that the drugs they need are not in stock, or that they cannot afford to wait. Other time costs include those for taking medication or treating oneself or one's children (e.g. preparing and giving oral rehydration salts solutions for diarrhoea). Consider household costs further by completing exercise 8A, page 130.

The term "cost" of health care is sometimes used to refer to problems suffered by people who cannot obtain care or who use poor-quality services. These problems can obviously include pain, worry and disability or death for the sufferer. These difficulties are better thought of as negative benefits—that is, failures to receive the benefits of care—rather than costs. The discussion here is limited to the cost of providing and obtaining health services. The large and complicated topic of benefits (or "costs" where benefits are negative) is not considered.

Why measure household costs?

One basic reason for measuring household costs—at least, in some studies—is to obtain a better understanding of user behaviour. To be useful, services must be *used*. Knowing the costs that householders bear if they use a service may help you to predict whether and how much the service will be used, or explain why it will not.

People will decide whether to seek a service for themselves or for someone in their household on the basis of its expected value. If they have to walk too far, or wait too long, or pay too high a price (assuming that fees are to be considered as "household costs"), they may decide against seeking some or all of the possible services. Where there are alternative types of care, such as traditional healers, the relative costs and benefits of these will enter into the decision.

Several factors appear likely to influence the anticipated satisfaction that patients receive from health services. They include the availability of drugs, the qualifications and attitudes of the staff, the sophistication of the equipment and the perceived success of previous contacts with the service. Some studies suggest that perceived quality of service is more important than fees when consumers are choosing a health service. Patients may avoid convenient but suspect health services in order to obtain treatment they prefer elsewhere.

If fee setting is being considered for your programme, you might try to obtain the following information about your target population:

- the average household income;
- the amount the population is willing to pay for specified services for the household;
- the percentage of average household income and the cost per head that would be represented by the estimated cost of providing certain services (or the entire programme).

You may be able to think of other information you would like to have. It is worth repeating, though, that household costs will only need to be considered in a few cost studies, so you may not often need to seek the above data.

While understanding user behaviour is one basic reason for looking at household costs, another is to try to minimize the cost of health care to society as a whole—in order to make sure that all scarce resources, including consumers' time, are used to their best advantage. Often, some trade-off between producers' and consumers' costs is required. For example, the more health centres and outreach facilities there are, the more costly it is for the health programme, but the more convenient and less costly it is for the patients. Some compromise is necessary, and it is often not easy to decide on the optimum arrangement. Take a moment now to consider how you would balance the conflicting costs that you identified at the end of exercise 8A (page 130).

Sometimes there are clear cases where failure to consider the users of health services leads to decisions that impose unnecessary costs on them. For example, a common phenomenon in many health facilities throughout the world is queues of patients, sometimes waiting for treatment for several hours in uncomfortable and crowded conditions.

Sometimes this situation is caused by a lack of resources at the centre. However, very often a few simple changes (at minimal cost to the health centre) could substantially reduce waiting times and discomfort of patients. These changes may include redistribution of staff, rationalization of procedures so that people do not have to move in a series of queues, providing a few shaded benches, and perhaps changing opening hours.

A study in India found the following: If in one week eight patients came from a particular village for treatment, the cost to them would be 64 rupees for transport (hire of a bullock cart at Rs 8 per day), a total of Rs 80 for drugs (the patients being on average slightly more sick than if they had been treated at home), and Rs 32 in wages lost (Rs 2 per day for patient and accompanying relative). If, on the other hand, the mobile team visited the village to treat the same patients, the cost of transport would be Rs 20 and the cost of drugs Rs 20.5. In this case, it was demonstrated that the mobile team would save household costs and apparently delivery-system (producers') costs as well.

Higher costs to the users of health services are sometimes reflected in cost-effectiveness measures, which will be studied more closely in Module 9. If the cost to patients goes over some threshold, patients may stop using the facility, attendance will fall, and the cost per person treated may well increase while resources will be underused.

If you attempt to combine health provider costs and household costs to compare them in different interventions, it is important to avoid double-counting. In some cases, the costs of the health service are shifted directly to the householder. For example, if fees are charged for drugs, you should not count them both as a cost to the health programme and as a cost to the householder. If the patient is paying $0.50 for a drug that costs the health service $2.50 to provide, the total cost to society of the drug is $2.50, not $3.00.

How to measure household costs

If you are interested only in the costs of *using* health services (or a particular service), you can study the individuals who attend health centres, hospitals (if they are involved in your programme) and other facilities. You could interview a sample of patients, asking them about the household costs associated with their current use of the facilities and also about previous visits. You could ask them their reasons for using (or not using) a particular facility rather than available alternatives, and how satisfied they have been with the quality of care. Staff members at the facility might be a good supplementary source for certain information, such as the probable cost in time to the patients of visiting each facility and waiting there. Another source of information would be patient records, which may yield useful data about drugs prescribed and the distance of patients' homes from the facility.

Of course, facility-based studies do not tell you anything about the costs to persons who did *not* use your programme for some of their services. To estimate these costs, you could sample other programmes to ask similar questions to the above, but that is not commonly done. Even if you do sample other programmes, if you wish to learn the relative importance of each of the different options (and, indeed, that of having no treatment at all), you must also do a household survey. Household surveys, requiring visits to people's homes, are difficult and expensive; they should be done only if the results are likely to influence the future direction of your programme and if you have the time and funds necessary to conduct them. Before you start on such a survey, think carefully about how the results could influence future health service design.

You cannot realistically expect that reading this manual will make you into a specialist in household surveys. If a survey has not already been conducted by, for example, an external donor or university, you may want to seek advice or help from specialists, e.g. in a government department or local university. For a quick practice in using household survey data, see exercise 8B, page 130.

Whether or not you are able to use actual survey data and other detailed information on household costs, make a point in your cost study reports of describing such costs qualitatively, so that you do not lose sight of them. This will protect you against the danger of "allowing the quantified to drive out the important". For some purposes, *all* costs count.

Cost-effectiveness analysis

Cost-effectiveness analysis is a technique to assist you in decision-making. It is one of the tools available to help you to identify areas of your health programme that are inefficient and to help you to design a better programme. A cost-effectiveness study involves assessing the gains (effectiveness) and resource input requirements (costs) of alternative ways of achieving a specified objective. The results are usually expressed in terms of cost per unit of effectiveness for each alternative. The alternative with the lowest cost per unit of effectiveness is the most cost-effective and is generally to be preferred on grounds of economic efficiency.

This technique can be applied to a whole range of questions that face managers of health programmes: from broad issues (e.g. which PHC programme to invest more funds in) to debates about specific details, such as the most suitable length for a training course.

A cost-effectiveness study should be done, if possible, whenever you are faced with a choice of options. It may not always be worth doing a rigorous analysis, but the general approach is worth following. Perhaps more money has become available and you need to decide where best to spend it; perhaps you have a new idea about where your programme should be going and need to convince others of its merits; perhaps you are evaluating the outcome of a programme and recognize that the evaluation provides an excellent opportunity to do a cost-effectiveness analysis.

A wide variety of issues can be examined in this way. They include, among others, choices of technology (e.g. choice of drugs for maternal and child health care activity or choice of pump for a water supply project), choices of delivery strategy (e.g. hospital versus clinic treatment of diarrhoeal disease), and choices of target (e.g. tetanus toxoid immunization for pregnant women or for all women of childbearing age). Although the issues addressed and the programmes involved can be quite diverse, there are five steps that are required for every cost-effectiveness analysis. Stated in terms of a programme, they involve:

- defining the programme's objectives;
- identifying the possible ways of achieving those objectives;
- identifying and measuring the costs of each option;
- identifying and measuring the effectiveness of each option;
- calculating the cost-effectiveness of each option and interpreting the results.

Define the objectives of the programme

The incentive for doing a cost-effectiveness study often comes from identifying a particular problem: for example, drugs are not readily available in rural areas, or contraceptive use in the communities is low, or malnutrition is common in children. In formulating the problem, you will usually automatically imply what the desired objective of the programme is. For example, the problem "contraceptive use in the communities is low" implies that your objective is "to increase contraceptive use" for various possible reasons.

It is usually helpful to refine the statement of the problem by exploring the nature of the possible causes, which might be suggested to you by experience and by past evaluation reports. For example, you may discover that contraceptives are not available in the health centres and conclude that this is probably the reason why contraceptive use is low. So you reformulate the problem as "inadequate supplies of contraceptives" and the objective as "increasing supplies of contraceptives to health centres". You may find that malnutrition seems to be a consequence of feeding children the wrong foods at the weaning stage, so your objective would be to encourage the use of better weaning foods.

The more precise your statement of objectives, the easier it is to use cost-effectiveness analysis, because both the costs and effects are likely to be more clearly defined and easier to measure and interpret. Specify the objectives quantitatively if possible: for example, "to reduce mortality from tetanus by 25%". It is normally easier if objectives expressed in percentage terms are translated into numbers. For example, if there are currently 400 tetanus deaths per year, the objective becomes to avert 100 deaths.

Cost-effectiveness studies may also be stimulated by a particular objective being set for you; for instance, the Ministry of Health informs you that it wishes to increase contraceptive coverage. It may simply wish to know whether the way you are currently doing something (e.g. distributing contraceptives) is the most efficient, or whether there may be better ways of doing it.

The objectives you are aiming for will depend not only on the type of programme you are involved in (for example, maternal and child health, education or disease control) and the sort of problems that emerge from it, but also on the scope of your responsibilities. Administrators at different levels are faced with different kinds of questions and objectives. A national manager might need to decide which type of refrigerator to use for the national vaccination cold chain. A district manager may be considering whether to use mobile or fixed facilities for distribution. The head of a health centre may wish to investigate how staff time should be allocated. In some cases at any level, data can be found to show how well the ultimate objective of health programmes—improving health status (i.e. reducing mortality or morbidity)—is being achieved.

For a start on practical cost-effectiveness work of your own, see exercise 9A, page 132.

Identify the possible ways of achieving the objectives

You need to identify at least two possible ways of achieving the objectives you have identified. A single cost-effectiveness result on its own tells you very little about efficiency. Consider the following example. A research worker undertook a cost-effectiveness study of treatment for a certain disease and found that a particular drug cost $20 per patient treated. What did that tell him about whether it was worth while to use that drug? Very little, without some basis for comparison. Investigation of the two most likely alternative drugs to treat the same disease revealed a cost of $100 per patient for each. After that, the researcher could begin to make some judgements about the merits of the first drug on efficiency grounds. For each option identified, be sure to describe it in sufficient detail. You may want to go back later and attempt to identify the features that made some options more cost-effective than others.

How do you identify suitable options? This will depend on whether your cost-effectiveness study is a response to the discovery of a particular problem, or is more exploratory. Each of these situations is explained and illustrated below.

Response to a problem

If the cost-effectiveness study is in response to the identification of a particular problem or issue, then the options you consider will represent the possible solutions you have identified for that problem. It is useful to consider a wide range of options at first, so as not to miss the best solution. When you have decided on your list of options, you should be careful to compare them with the best possible alternatives known to you, and not simply those that are being implemented at present. For example, take a country which currently imports brand-name drugs, and is considering whether to supplement or replace that approach by manufacturing drugs domestically. An analysis that simply compared domestic production with the current system (importing brand-name products) might suggest that domestic production is preferable. If, however, the possibility of importing generic drugs is also included in the cost-effectiveness analysis, the answer may be different. Including it may complicate the analysis, but would produce useful results.

Once you have generated an initial list of options, you probably need to be selective; a full cost-effectiveness analysis of all conceivable options is usually costly and unnecessary. You can narrow down the options to a manageable selection by *eliminating* those that:

- cannot be accommodated within the existing budget constraints;

- arc clearly less efficient than other options on the basis of a rough calculation of costs and effects;
- are not feasible in technical and political terms (consider all options that have powerful political support even if they are unworkable; if they really are poor options in economic terms, this needs to be carefully documented);
- cannot be analysed easily and cheaply in time to influence decision-making.

See exercise 9B, page 132, to apply some of these ideas.

Exploratory study

An exploratory study can involve comparing the performance of two or more approaches currently being used to meet some objective, or examining the expected performance of completely new approaches to an objective. The nature of the options is likely to be less clearly specified than for a problem-solving response. For example, you may decide simply to compare the way different health centres provide curative treatment or the way different districts distribute drugs. You may not have identified the specific characteristics that you think are likely to make one option more or less efficient. It may not be until you have studied a number of examples that you realize which characteristics are responsible for making some options more efficient. For example, you may find, after studying two immunization strategies, e.g. mass campaigns and routine services, that certain features (promotion through the mass media or more reliable refrigeration to prevent vaccine wastage) are among the crucial characteristics contributing to efficiency.

No matter how clearly specified the options may be at the start of your analysis, you may have to restrict the study to a few of them owing to limitations of funds and time. If so, you can narrow them down by focusing on the approaches that seem to use more resources and so might benefit more from any improvement in efficiency, or by selecting a mixture of some promising approaches and some weaker ones to see whether you can identify the key differences.

Identify and measure the costs of each option

For each of the options chosen for analysis, you will need to measure the costs. Guidelines for doing that have already been given (in Modules 4 and 6 for financial costs and Module 7 for economic costs). For assessment of true economic efficiency, economic costs will be needed.

There are some specific points to bear in mind when estimating costs for the purpose of cost-effectiveness analysis. For one thing, the cost and effectiveness measures must be linked for each alternative studied. The resources you are costing should be those that are responsible for producing the effects you will be measuring. Usually, this means that you should be measuring the costs and the effectiveness over approximately the same period of time, although for health status effects that require some time to appear, there would be a delay after the period when the programme's costs are incurred. Take a few minutes—without doing a full exercise—to think of examples where there are likely to be significant delays between using the resources and achieving an effect. How (and when) would you measure cost-effectiveness in such cases?

Another thing to stress about costs is the need to be comprehensive—that is, to include in your cost measurements all the inputs that are put to work in that option. Use the categories given in Module 1, page 6, as a checklist to ensure that you are not overlooking resources that should be included. When you think you have included all the relevant resources, check again by going through the list and identifying: (1) every relevant function; (2) every contributor; (3) every level at which the option is employed. Donations as well as paid-for resources should be included. However, in your efforts to be comprehensive for each alternative, take care not to count any resources more than once. If you use the input categories proposed, double-counting is unlikely.

Where a new service or set of services is being added to an existing programme—for instance, when a new vaccine (e.g. against hepatitis B virus) is being added to the existing national immunization programme—it will be sufficient to look only at the costs and effects of the new components. The method that economists usually prefer is to count only the additional or incremental costs (which they would call "marginal costs") of the new component. In a different situation, two or more options may differ from each other in only a few of the inputs used; in this case, only the costs (and effects) of those inputs need to be compared. However, by doing this, you run the risk of overlooking other differences, and obscuring the exact meaning of the cost-effectiveness indicator. It is therefore probably wiser to include the costs of *all* inputs for each option.

Identify and measure the effectiveness of each option

Module 5 covers measures of effectiveness at some length. Review it to remind yourself about the different types of measure and the qualities that make some better than others.

It is important to be sure that the effects you are measuring result from the resource inputs whose costs you are also calculating. Sometimes, identifying results (that is, determining cause and effect) is not easy. You should simply make the best judgements possible in each case.

Calculate and interpret the cost-effectiveness of each option

You can calculate the cost-effectiveness ratio for each option by dividing its cost by the numerical value of the chosen effect. The ratios are then compared to determine the most cost-effective option–that is, the one costing the least per unit of effect achieved.

Often it is necessary to make assumptions about some variables whose exact value is uncertain. These variables may be ones involved in calculations of either costs or effectiveness. For example, the planning ministry may not have a standard discount rate, so you may instead use a commercial interest rate or a World Bank figure as a proxy for capital costs. Or your estimates of the amount of time that staff devote to a particular programme may be only approximate (a fairly common problem). Or you may have a variable, such as a price, that has changed over time and you have used the average value. To deal with this kind of uncertainty for a particular assumption, define a plausible range of values for the variable, or take (1) your best estimate, (2) twice that estimate and (3) half of it. Taking each of these figures in turn (or using the values at either end of the plausible range), calculate how the results of your analysis change with the different values. If your conclusion as to the most cost-effective option changes, then the conclusions are said to be sensitive to your assumption about the value of that variable. The process of testing how changes in assumptions affect changes in results is called sensitivity analysis.

Having established which of the options is the most cost-effective, an important follow-up step is to decide what is responsible for the differences among them. This may guide you in modifying the design or improving the implementation of a programme. For example, having identified which health centres are the least cost-effective within a programme, you might then look in more detail at the factors responsible for this. You may find, for example, that health centres with a particular cadre of health worker are less efficient, or that some units are underused. You could follow this up with further studies looking specifically at the cost-effectiveness of different cadres of health workers, or at the cost implications of an inefficient use of staff time. Of course, the effects must remain comparable over time if this process is to be of any value.

Another possible follow-up is to study the cost profiles of the options under consideration. Which input categories account for a significantly different percentage of the total cost in the more cost-effective and less cost-effective options? Does this appear to explain the difference in cost-effectiveness? Can the least cost-effective option be improved by changing the way resources are used? All these possible influences on cost (and, thus, on cost-effectiveness) are discussed further in Module 12.

To interpret the results further, look at overall effectiveness. Could differences in scale explain the differences in cost-effectiveness? What would happen if the different options were scaled up or down? Is there a particular level of output that you wish to achieve? If so, it would be desirable to make adjustments to all the options in order to see what would happen if they were operating at that level. However, there is a potential problem here. There may be no straightforward relationship between changes in effect and scale and it will not always be easy to formulate policies based on the adjustment and retesting suggested here. You will probably have a good idea when it is safe to do so and when it is not. (These issues are discussed further in part C.)

A third way of interpreting your results is to study the different conditions under which the different options were operating (i.e. geography, population distribution and other variables). Do any of these help to explain the differences in cost-effectiveness?

The translation of inputs into effectiveness often goes through a series of stages. For example, the provision of water and sanitation facilities can be expected to influence health only if: (1) the facilities are working; (2) they are being used; (3) they are being used properly. Try to identify the key stages in the transformation process for your programme. At what stage do the differences between the options become obvious? For example, is it differences in the functioning, frequency of use or quality of use of the different sanitation options that best explains the differences in cost-effectiveness of different sanitation technologies? You will need to carry out an analysis at each of these stages if the answer to the basic question is not obvious from your examination of the conditions and the study results.

To get a better feel for what is involved in cost-effectiveness analyses, including interpretation of their results, do exercises 9C and 9D, pages 133–135.

Using cost data in planning

MODULE 10

Future costs

Predicting the future is never easy. But it is important to make the best guesses one can. One important illustration of predictions is a budget. Budgets are documents that set out the activities planned for the future and outline the expected future costs of the programme (and of programme subdivisions). The process surrounding the development of a budget can be quite complicated. It involves a whole series of activities, including: identifying needs, establishing priorities, setting targets, designing programmes to meet those targets, esti- mating the costs of the programmes, fixing an upper limit on expenditure, deciding who should be involved in developing the budget and drawing up a timetable to show when discussions, submissions and budget approvals should take place.

This module does not attempt to explore all these issues in detail. We will focus instead on one of them — the method of estimating future costs — and on the uses to which budgets can be put in deciding what health programmes to implement.

How to estimate future costs

The method of estimating the likely future costs of a health programme has many features in common with the method of measuring existing costs covered in Modules 4 and 7. For one thing, the same framework is appropriate: resources (and costs) can be classified according to type of input, the activity they are used for, who is expected to contribute to them, and what kind of currency is involved. Use the checklists in Module 1 to guide you in adapting the framework to budgets.

Also, as with existing programmes, you need to identify clearly the health services whose future costs you wish to estimate. In particular, this means you must:

- Describe the proposed programme in as much detail as possible.
- Examine the resources that already exist and determine whether they have the capacity to take on additional tasks (i.e. is there any spare capacity?).
- Determine the *additional* (incremental or marginal) resources required.

Cost estimation for a future programme has other features in common with that for existing programmes. It is sometimes appropriate to estimate in detail a sample of the activities of the planned future programme and extrapolate from these to the full programme. It is also important to distinguish between financial costs (money outlay) and economic costs. (You will often want to estimate both types of costs.)

However, there are a number of areas where differences in emphasis or procedures emerge. For example, in the choice of the future time period, you have considerably greater flexibility than is possible when measuring the actual costs of an existing programme. Actual costs rely on information on use and expenditure: there are often delays in gaining access to this information, and its usability deteriorates over time. Information can become obsolete quite quickly, and you should always be careful when using historic data for projections. Future costs do not face these problems. It is usually appropriate to estimate future costs for a period of 5–10 years. Naturally, the time period selected will depend on your specific needs.

There are three general approaches to estimating future costs (both economic and financial). Sometimes it is possible to use them in combination. These approaches are explained below.

The "ingredients" approach

The "ingredients" approach involves translating the general description of whatever programme is to be costed into specific resource requirements. To do this, you should list in detail the number and types of staff, the number and types of vehicles, the quantity and types of drugs, and so forth. Calculate the cost for each item by multiplying the quantity by the price, and then add up all the individual costs.

For the whole programme (or for each identified activity of the programme) you would prepare a detailed list of all the resources required, the quantities of each resource, the unit price, and (for capital items) the expected life of the item. For *each* year of the proposed programme (at least five years for a long-term programme), you would fill in the details of resource requirements as indicated in the table below, to which details for all the "ingredients" of each input category must be added.

Consider the "ingredients" approach further by doing exercise 10A, page 136.

The "ingredients" approach requires a thorough understanding of the resources required for a new project. Specifying the details of planned project implementation can be a very useful exercise for the good design and management of programmes. For this reason, it is recommended that you start by using the "ingredients" approach when estimating future costs.

This approach is particularly appropriate to use when:

- the programme to be costed is new or rapidly changing, and existing programme costs may not provide a reliable guide;

Cost estimation for long-term budget preparation — year____

Input	Description (type and unit of measure)	Quantity (number of units) Q	Price per unit P	Useful life	Annualization factor A^*	Annualized cost $\dfrac{Q \times P}{A}$
Capital						
Vehicles						
Equipment						
Buildings, space						
Training, non-recurrent						
Social mobilization, non-recurrent						
Subtotal, capital						
Recurrent						
Personnel						
Supplies						
Vehicles, operation & maintenance						
Buildings, operation & maintenance						
Training, recurrent						
Social mobilization, recurrent						
Other operating inputs						
Subtotal, recurrent						
Total						

*Annualization factor = 1.0 for all recurrent costs.

- the available cost data are incomplete or unreliable, and it is feasible to document the resources required in some detail.

Unfortunately, for many health projects detailed resource requirements are difficult to predict. Losses of supplies will occur to a greater or lesser extent, affecting the full cost of delivering the planned services. The combination or mix of personnel employed, even at the basic delivery unit level, may change over time in unexpected ways. (The substitution of a community health worker for a physician or nurse for certain tasks is a case in point.) The ratio of labour to equipment or other resources may be equally unpredictable.

Perhaps not surprisingly, estimates of future costs that rely on itemizing resources tend to focus on the items of large cost (mostly capital items, which are discussed in earlier modules). Much less attention is likely to be paid to estimating recurrent costs. This is unfortunate for several reasons:

- The items classified under recurrent costs, although often of low individual value, are frequently purchased in large amounts and thus can contribute significantly to overall costs.
- Inadequate funding for recurrent costs is likely to jeopardize the effectiveness of the whole programme. Recurrent items are often complementary to capital inputs. Many capital items, such as vehicles and equipment, will not function adequately without, for example, fuel or power or maintenance.
- Recurrent costs are usually borne by recipient governments in developing countries, even when outside donors provide capital items such as equipment or vehicles, and the government is likely to have limited flexibility to provide more resources if the initial budget is incorrect.

Because detailed documentation of resources is tedious (particularly for recurrent costs) and there is a danger that some costs will be left out, a second approach, described below, has some advantages.

The "adaptation" approach

This second approach to prediction involves using your experience of what a certain kind of programme actually costs to estimate what a similar programme planned for the future might cost. This has the advantage of accommodating not only obvious recurrent costs but also wastage and other costs which might easily be overlooked in the "ingredients" approach. This second method shares with the first the difficulty of allowing for changes in the proportions of resource inputs employed, but it has some advantages.

The "adaptation" approach involves the following steps:

- Select a programme that (a) is as similar as possible to the planned one; (b) operates as rationally and efficiently as the planned one is likely to; (c) has accessible cost data.
- Estimate the costs of that programme, using Modules 4 and 7 as guides or making use of available estimates.
- Adjust your estimates to take into account any known differences between the programme costed and the planned programme.

One of the major challenges is to know how to modify appropriately the cost data you have. One important difference that is likely to exist between the costed programme and the one you are planning is size. Total costs are likely to be misleading in this case. As a first approximation, you will need to know unit costs, such as total cost per contact, per facility and per district. Which of these is most relevant will depend on the aspects of the costed (current or past) programme you are going to reproduce. For example, if you are establishing similar health centres in another area, you might use cost per facility (and multiply this by the number of planned new facilities to get the total future cost estimate). If you are expanding the catchment areas of existing facilities, cost per contact would be more appropriate. If you are establishing a similar programme in a new district, cost per district may be the most useful guide, assuming a reasonable similarity between the two populations served in terms of size and demographic structure.

Often, you will have to make adjustments to take into account the existing infrastructure. For example, your planned programme may not need additional buildings, but the cost data available might include building costs. In that case, if possible, you would eliminate building costs from the estimates. In other words, for budgetary purposes you do not want the average *total* cost of the existing programme, but the average *additional* or incremental costs of the new one.

Even if it is difficult to find programmes that are very similar to the planned one, you may be able to make use of some parts of existing cost estimates. In particular, you should use available cost data to help estimate the likely recurrent costs associated with capital investments. Usually, it is relatively easy to work out what capital inputs your new programme requires (using the "ingredients" approach), for example the number of vehicles and the number of refrigerators. You could then use available cost data on the relationship between capital inputs and their recurrent costs (the "adaptation" approach). You could look at the recurrent cost for each capital item. For example, expenditure data for existing programmes could give you an estimate of the average annual cost of running a vehicle (i.e. the operation and maintenance cost per vehicle). This could save you the difficult (and probably unreliable) exercise of attempting to document all the different running costs a vehicle is likely to have (fuel, oil, spare parts, registration, insurance). Your existing cost data may show you that, on average, it costs about $ 800 a year to operate a vehicle, and you could apply this estimate to your future programme.

Even with such information, you should not assume that it is appropriate to apply costs from one situation directly to another. For example, the running costs for a vehicle in a city are likely to be very different from those for the same vehicle used on poorly maintained rural roads. Or maintenance might have been inadequately funded. Fortunately, it is usually easier to understand the factors that influence the value of a specific category of costs than it is to understand those that influence total costs, so that you can often make appropriate adjustments.

In general, use the "adaptation" approach when:

- the programmes for which cost data are available are broadly representative of the planned programmes;
- the programmes costed have been adequately funded and have functioned efficiently (check, for example, that supplies of fuel and drugs have been adequate);
- costs for existing programmes can be reasonably readily obtained (i.e. more easily than documenting resource requirements in detail as in the "ingredients" approach).

The "mark-up" approach

For programmes that are already under way, a third, and very common, way of estimating future costs is simply to add a certain percentage to cost estimates from the recent past—a kind of "mark-up" of past values. This might be an arbitrary percentage, perhaps just taking into account expected inflation.

The danger with this approach is that it assumes that the programme has been adequate in the past, and discourages consideration of new initiatives or modifications. It also depends on reasonably accurate past cost estimates for the programme. However, a very detailed estimate of future costs will not be needed every year. Once a programme has been initiated, it is often necessary only to:

- determine current and recent costs of the programme (i.e. take stock);
- modify these estimates to reflect general cost trends, e.g. by using official price indexes, and allow for demographic changes, health service developments and any special problems expected to arise;
- check annually that expenditure is in line with the budgets, and adjust the budget if necessary;
- prepare a detailed budget to incorporate any new items into the programme.

How to use future cost estimates for decision-making

Assuming that you have used one or a combination of the three approaches outlined above to estimate future costs, you are ready to go on to use the information. The uses of cost estimates for possible future activities are essentially the same as those for existing programmes, described in the Introduction and Module 2 to compare costs with available resources and measure efficiency, equity and priorities. But there is one crucial difference, which stems from the fact that, if information is going to be useful for decision-making, it has to say something about the future. (This point was made briefly in Module 2, in the section entitled "Making cost projections", page 16.)

Retrospective costings can help to determine how appropriate previous decisions were (in other words, were past programmes affordable, efficient and equitable?). However, they are limited in how much they can tell us about what should be done to *improve* a situation. They may highlight possible problems and areas to focus attention on (e.g. by showing where most resources are currently spent), but they cannot give any firm guidelines about appropriate modifications. Much of their value will depend on what they can tell us about activities that have not yet been implemented. Retrospective cost calculations should be made with one eye on the future, for their relevance to new or revised programmes. Good information on the past, whatever the verdict it suggests on *previous* programmes, can be helpful for the things to come in the health system—at the level of the community as well as nationally.

A decision to invest resources in a new programme will be based on many considerations. As part of the decision-making process, you can use projections of costs to help to answer two crucial questions: (1) Is the programme affordable? and (2) Is it likely to be efficient?

Affordability

A health programme is affordable if, and only if, each of the parties who must contribute to financing its operation is able and willing to do so, both at the outset and later on. To analyse affordability, financial costs matter more than economic ones (although changes in patterns of support may blur that distinction).

If the total finances required to implement a programme are not available when needed, the programme's effectiveness will be reduced, sometimes seriously. Imagine a hospital whose construction is complete but where there are no funds for staff: it is practically useless. It is very important to make sure in advance that finances will be available to implement the programme well. Nothing in the future can ever be certain, of course, but at least you should have a reasonable expectation of finding the funds for whatever new development or expansion is planned before you start.

Make a good estimate of the expected additional financial costs of your proposed programme—that is, its budget—for a period of up to ten years. If possible, use the input categories suggested throughout this manual, adapting them where necessary to the standard budgetary format of your organization. Pay particular attention to recurrent costs, which you will need to keep under constant control. Nonrecurrent costs cannot be avoided, either, owing to the need for replacement. You must not forget that the recurrent cost burden often changes when an old capital item is replaced by a new one. For all categories of costs, distinguish in your budget between financing in cash and resources likely to be donated in kind (e.g. vaccines supplied and paid for by external agencies).

Certain adjustments, e.g. for inflation or changes in foreign exchange rates, can be incorporated in the budget process (in addition to the customary contingency allowances), especially at higher levels of care. This can also be done at lower levels, provided that appropriate technical advice is readily available. For one thing, a budget will need to make allowances for inflation. This is where economic specialists can be useful. No one can be sure of the future, but experts can probably help you to go beyond simple extrapolations of past price increases when building inflation allowances into your budget.

Even more technical—and more likely to be determined at national level—are matters involving foreign exchange. For each year of your budget, you should try to separate local currency from foreign currency requirements for financing inputs. It is necessary to make this distinction for a number of reasons:

- In some countries, access to foreign exchange may be limited (i.e. the budget constraint is more severe), so separate planning is needed.
- Foreign exchange rates vary over time. This will affect the amount of local currency needed to purchase foreign exchange inputs. For each year, identify which resources requiring foreign exchange will be paid for locally, and calculate each cost in local currency, using a range of estimates of likely foreign exchange rates. (Recent rates can be found in the periodical *International financial statistics*, published by the International Monetary Fund, but you should not hesitate to seek assistance from local specialists when necessary.)

Estimates of future costs, especially those made at higher levels where economic and other information is more complete, may include special data on the source of funds and the form of resources provided. In such cases, it will be useful to list all possible sources of finance (Ministry of Health and other government bodies, consumers, donors) and how much each is likely to provide. Prepare a separate sub-budget for each major contributor, and indicate how firm their commitment is. Comment on the consequences of any failure to provide specified resources. In particular, consider how likely it is that donors will continue to provide the same level of funding in the long term. Look at trends in expenditure in previous years and at the donor's previous practice, if known. What alternative sources are there if the current donors do not continue to support the programme? Calculate the proportion of costs borne by donors to obtain some indication of the likelihood of the programme becoming unafford-able.

Suppose that your calculations and projections suggest that insufficient funds will be available for the programme. If that problem is still evident after you have checked the numbers, you will have three basic choices:

- *Modify the design of the new or revised programme.* Are there ways to make the original design more efficient? Can you operate on a smaller scale?

- *Find additional sources of finance.* Look first at the national financing system to see whether allocations could be increased. Then, consider bilateral or international assistance (from either governments or nongovernmental organizations). If you are involved in a major new programme, it may be necessary to consider user fees or other ways to tap more directly into available local resources.
- *Reject the programme design and consider alternative strategies.*

You should avoid submitting a proposal that would cost more than the currently available funds. Administrators unfamiliar with your programme may simply reduce some components arbitrarily. For example, with a proposal for an essential drugs programme that costs twice the funds available, the quantities of all drugs may simply be halved. Since not all drugs are of equal importance, a far better approach would be to submit a new drug list in keeping with the available finances, which provides for cuts in less essential drugs first, and in more essential ones only as a last resort.

Efficiency

A second important use for estimates of future costs is to select help you to select the most cost-effective solution from the ones that are financially affordable. For this judgement of efficiency, economic costs (see Module 7) should usually be used.

Cost-effectiveness analysis (see Module 9) is one useful approach for identifying the most efficient options. The only difference in methodology when considering future programmes is that, instead of calculating cost-effectiveness for one particular year, you can determine the average over the life of the programme, or at least over several years. Because of the variable life of capital items and the importance of time in estimating value, the procedure of discounting is used to express all costs (and effects) in their equivalent values for the present year. (When a proper discount rate is used in assessing efficiency, it will not be necessary to make adjustments for inflation.)

The procedure for discounting is as follows. Choose a base year (say, the first year of the proposed programme). The value of items, including capital items, purchased in that year remains unchanged. However, the real value of goods purchased in the second year must be discounted by a relevant discount rate (similar to the process described in Module 7). If the discount rate is 10%, $ 1000 spent in year 2 is equivalent to $ 910 in year 1 ($ 1000/(1 + 0.10)). Goods purchased in the third year are discounted a further 10%, and so on. The calculation is essentially the reverse of calculating compound interest. The result of this process is to yield a single "present value" figure for all costs (and effects). Just as for annualized capital costs, as explained in Module 7, there are standard tables of the factors needed to do the discounting. No such calculation is required at this point in the manual.

As noted above, you will be looking for economic costs in most analyses of efficiency. As a rough guide to calculating these completely, consider the following guidelines:

- Take the financial costs, and add your estimates of the value of the additional resources that will not require financing, such as the cash equivalents (per year) of existing capital items and of donated resources.
- Estimate the value of resources diverted to your purposes from other productive activities (for example, staff who are already employed and who will be asked to give up some other responsibilities to work on your project).
- Consider the appropriateness of the prices that you have used to calculate wages, and consider the probable value of foreign exchange as it will affect certain inputs, making any necessary adjustments to your preliminary cost estimates.

Although the assessment of health programme efficiency in planning for the future may seem rather complicated from the description given here, it is often feasible and well worth the effort required, because it will allow better health care from a given budget. Exercise 10B, page 136, offers a further insight into some of the essential ideas.

Financial analysis

This module briefly reviews some important applications of cost data in financial analysis, using existing and projected values of the costs and effects of primary health care. Some of the information given here expands on that given in earlier modules.

Naturally, the possible applications of cost data will depend on the availability of sufficient data and the reliability of those data, which, in turn, depend on the methods of collection and interpretation of information. Other severe constraints include the time and funds available to explore applications.

The data and applications discussed here will be of interest mainly to higher-level health officials. However, planning below the national level is an important subject for the manual as a whole, so we have included some brief reminders here for district-level personnel. You will recall the coverage in Module 2 of comparisons between expected budget and actual expenditure, which require frequent application in every programme at every level. You could refer to table 2.1, page 18, with its associated questions and to exercises 2A and 2D(b). Also important to district health officials and others serving at levels below the central one is the projection of available information into the future for budgetary and other purposes. (See the explanations, examples and exercises in Module 10.) This module reviews and extends the applications of analyses of cost and cost-effectiveness to the following topics: differences between various levels of the health system; equity; affordability; and cost recovery.

Applications at different levels of the health system

The cost data available to health personnel will necessarily vary somewhat by level. Some of the variability is obvious. For example, only national officials are in a position to know central office costs (not to mention the many sources of finance, including external assistance). Local officials, on the other hand, are in the best position to know about staffing ratios, while the people actually delivering services in facilities may be the only ones aware of any difference between the time allocated for certain tasks and that actually worked by staff members.

Equally, information on the effects of health care will vary by level. As explained in Modules 5 and 9, there are many measures of effectiveness. Local personnel will usually have access to primary data on service outputs and perhaps to changes in the attitudes and behaviour of patients. At the other extreme, if health status outcomes can be estimated at all, it will very likely be only through efforts made at national (or perhaps regional) level.

Thus, cost-effectiveness studies may differ between levels, or require cooperation throughout the health system. Both the uses of such studies and the implications of results for further research are described in detail in Module 9. It should be evident in your work which kinds of studies of costs and cost-effectiveness will be feasible for district-level planning and administration.

Equity

Equity in health service delivery (who receives care ?) and in the financing of care (who pays for it ?) is a vital objective. Its general relation to cost analysis has been described briefly in Modules 2, 7 and 8.

While there can be little dispute over the desirability of an equitable health system, securing enough information on equity to be able to influence policies and practices is not easy. The widespread need for more and better health care in most developing countries justifies attempts to try to identify both those who receive care and those who pay for it, distinguishing between them in terms of economic status, sex, geographical location and so forth. There are various possible measures of equity—referring, for instance, to availability and use of services (including use in relation to the need for care)—and most of these require data derived from households. It is necessary to find out who does *not* receive care as well as who does, and to determine the characteristics of users and non-users. Unfortunately, household data are often not available and are difficult to obtain, as explained in Module 8.

You can, however, try to find (or collect) and put to use information on target populations and on expenditure made by and for them to obtain health care. Two aspects of such efforts are explored in exercises 11A and 11B, page 139, which extend earlier exercises. Try them before moving on to the next section.

Affordability

Affordability was discussed in Module 10. To build on the information given there, do exercise 11C, page 140.

Cost recovery

In Module 10, we noted that, if a programme is not affordable, health officials have three basic options: (1) to modify the programme; (2) to find additional sources of funds; (3) to reject the programme and turn to other strategies. The second of these choices often involves recovering programme costs, through various possible means, such as user charges (fees). Decisions on such changes are usually made at the highest level of the system, but health personnel at all levels will be concerned with the policies and especially the ways in which they are administered. (Details of collecting and spending fees are beyond the scope of this manual.)

Some guidelines on cost recovery, including user charges, are provided in Module 2, which raises the important point of possible problems connected with patients' ability to pay leading to potential threats to equity. Module 8 develops that theme and notes the difficulties of obtaining information for an adequate assessment of ability—as well as willingness—to pay for care. It is worth looking again at exercise 8B, page 130, as you complete this brief review of cost recovery applications in financial analysis.

MODULE 12

Managerial efficiency

The use of cost findings to assess the efficiency of health service delivery has been covered in Modules 2, 6, 7 and 9. Here, these approaches to improving the efficiency of delivery units are developed further for consideration by facility managers and their supervisors.

To achieve greater efficiency, especially at the community level, it is necessary to investigate how total and unit costs differ among facilities at a given time, and how they vary for the same facility over time. Analysing these costs to find the factors that affect them is not easy, especially when concepts such as quality of care and the possible effects of population characteristics and geographical variables are taken into account. Nevertheless, major cost differences at "outliers" (sites that stand out at one extreme or the other) can be particularly worthy of investigation.

What total cost profiles reveal about efficiency

As explained in Module 2, the total cost of a programme or of certain activities at a particular delivery facility is often broken down into its separate components to show resource inputs. Each category of input can be expressed as a monetary value and as a percentage of the total. Lessons may be learned from the profile of costs over time or—probably more useful—when there are differences between sites. The large cost category of personnel is worth examining for unusual percentage values, and drugs and vehicles are categories where notable differences are often to be found. If one health centre in a district or region stands out because of its very high drug costs, for example, it should be examined further by its manager and supervisors (as explained in Module 2). Studies of PHC costs at the local level in many countries have revealed considerable variations in the use of pharmaceuticals and in their cost per patient contact, leading in some cases to reviews of drug supply and prescribing practices.

Another illustration of the efficiency "messages" conveyed by cost data is a situation where an unexpectedly high share of total costs in an immunization programme is found to be attributable to purchase of vaccines. High wastage rates might be involved; this must be determined by closer inspection of the programme.

For a major PHC programme, the nationwide profiles of two similar African countries showed a considerable difference in the personnel percentages of the cost profiles. This led to a consideration of various possible explanations. In this case, different rates of pay for staff appeared to be a major factor, while no differences either in the total number employed or in staffing ratios (e.g. the ratio of physicians to nurses) were evident. (Conversely, studies in other countries have found major differences in staffing ratios across health centres.) These cost factors and others are considered further in the following section.

Some important influences on average costs and their implications for efficiency

What are the most common factors affecting total and, more importantly, average costs? Identifying these can provide useful lessons for improving health programme efficiency. Briefly, it might be worth examining average costs to learn whether any of the following appears to have had a significant influence:

- prices paid for inputs;
- staffing ratios;
- staff productivity;
- intensity of use of a facility (volume of care in relation to capacity);
- economies of scale (cost savings from a larger capacity of the facility);
- economies of scope (cost savings from a greater diversity of services).

The possible importance of some of these factors does not require much explanation here. For example, it is clear that, if input prices can be controlled without reduction in quality, the efficiency of service delivery will be higher. Data on most such prices are likely to be readily available. As another example, staffing ratios, e.g. the ratio of physicians to nurses or of registered nurses to aides can affect the cost per unit of service at a facility. Examining the ratios for different facilities may reveal some unusual patterns that have inflated costs; if so, there may be opportunities for increasing efficiency by changing the ratios. Of course, your ability to do this will depend on whether or not the health system offers you sufficient flexibility in handling staffing. Opportunities to make such changes may be greater in hospitals than at primary care sites.

Staff productivity inevitably affects the average cost of services, and hence the efficiency of providing them. Other things being equal, when a staff member (e.g. a nurse) generates a higher output per day (e.g. makes more home visits), the unit cost falls. Of course, there can be counteracting influences. The nurse's productivity may rise because there are additional supporting personnel and equipment in the centre. The overall effect on average cost is unpredictable, and would have to be checked. In a Latin American cost study, two different PHC programmes were compared; one showed an appreciably lower cost per visit than the other did for seemingly comparable patients. Inspection of the data showed that the more cost-effective programme actually had lower productivity indicating a need to search for other explanations for cost differences.

The intensity of use of a health care facility, that is, the volume of service provided in relation to the facility's full capacity, is a logical cost determinant; for a higher volume (or percentage of capacity used), fixed costs are spread over more output, reducing the cost per unit of service. This has been demonstrated in a variety of PHC programmes, so it is worth considering whenever cost results are being interpreted to assess efficiency. If you find much unused capacity in some or all of the facilities of your programme, you may want to re-examine the number and location of delivery sites and the frequency of treatment sessions.

You may very well have heard someone attribute a local delivery site's comparatively low average costs to "economies of scale". An economist would use this term to mean that larger facilities can produce services at lower unit cost. This is plausible, but it is not always true: there is such a thing as being *too large* for good managerial control. If you have enough information, you could try to compare the average costs of facilities of different size (assuming comparable intensities of use) for certain services. To show the need for caution in expecting economies of scale, one study of the national immunization programmes in two developing countries found that smaller facilities in both appeared to have *lower* costs per dose of vaccine administered.

A final cost factor suggested here for your consideration is "economy of scope". It refers to possible savings in average costs from providing a wider range of different services at the same facility, i.e. other things being equal, a health centre that provides a large number of different types of services can produce each of them at lower unit cost. Among the explanations is the more efficient use of the centre's administration, building and other facilities, which reduces the overhead costs of each service. Some, but not all, studies looking at economies of scope, e.g. the one in Latin America cited above, have found them. Where data and time permit, it may be worth while to test the possible gains in efficiency from providing a wider range of services.

Conclusion

Exercise 12A, page 141, which applies some of the above ideas, completes this module. We hope that the discussion here has shown you the potential value of certain specific steps to assess and promote efficiency in health service delivery. This use of cost analysis can complement other uses, such as planning and budgeting.

You should by now be familiar with the basic concepts of cost analysis— including financial cost, economic cost and effectiveness—as well as with the most important ways of making the appropriate measurements. You are now ready to apply these concepts in the evaluation of programmes and facilities in your own country.

Exercises

Some notes on computations

For many of the exercises in the following pages, you will need to do some computations. You may need to calculate, for example, various components of costs and to add them together to arrive at totals for a health programme or service delivery facility. You will also have to do some basic cost-effectiveness calculations to decide, for example, the cost per death prevented by immunizations. Some of this computational work may seem very detailed, but the mathematics involved is straightforward. You will find it helpful to use a hand calculator to do some of the exercises.

The question of using computers is bound to come up. For this type of cost analysis, a computer is *not* required. Anyone who has experience with personal computers and spreadsheet programmes will see places where they could be used, and they could in the long run be very productive. However, this manual has been designed to be used without such aids.

When you come to do actual analyses of your programme or facility, feel free to use any computational aids that are available to you. Perhaps you or a member of your staff will use a spreadsheet programme on a personal computer at that time. It will be important to share your experiences of different computational approaches, so that others too can learn about further applications of cost analysis.

EXERCISES FOR MODULE 1

■ Exercise 1A (time: 10 minutes)

List the different categories of resource inputs that you see in the picture.

What other categories of inputs exist for typical PHC programmes?

(Now return to the place in the manual where you were before doing the exercise.)

■ Exercise 1B (time: 20 minutes)

Relate the chart of costs by input categories on page 6 to a specific health programme for which you are responsible or have good knowledge. Do this by listing details of inputs in each category in the table opposite.

Input category	Details
Capital	
Vehicles	
Equipment	
Buildings, space	
Training, nonrecurrent	
Social mobilization, nonrecurrent	
Recurrent	
Personnel	
Supplies	
Vehicles, operation & maintenance	
Buildings, operation & maintenance	
Training, recurrent	
Social mobilization, recurrent	
Other operating inputs	

If you are using this manual in a training programme, compare your list with the list of another trainee, and discuss the difference between the two.

■ Exercise 1C (time: 10 minutes)

For the health programme that you dealt with in exercise 1B, record the major functions or activities involved in the programme and the resource inputs (in the categories used in exercise 1B) that are required for each.

Put your answers on a sheet of paper with headings like these:

Activity 1:_____
Inputs required:

Activity 2:_____
Inputs required:
etc.

■ Exercise 1D (time: 5 mInutes)

For the same programme, list any physical inputs or types of activities that usually involve foreign currency, identify the contributors (including the government) who provide them, and note the currencies used.

Inputs or activities involving foreign currency	Contributor	Currency

■ Exercise 1E (time: 45 minutes)

List the subdivisions ("heads" and "subheads") used in the budget documents for your programme, and note which of them represent physical inputs and which functions (activities).

Subdivision	Input or function?

Do you see any potential for overlap in any of the subdivisions? If so, in which?

If you were to transform your existing budget to make it compatible with the recommended list of inputs, which budgetary items would you combine? What new categories would you need to create?

Compare and contrast your answers on this exercise with those of another trainee.

■ Exercise 1F (time: 15 minutes)

Assume that you plan to implement a breast-feeding education programme in a hospital directed at women who have come to deliver their babies in hospital. Record below your answers to the following questions:

● What are the major activities that this programme is likely to involve?
● What kinds of physical inputs would be needed for each activity? (List their details quickly.)

Activity	Inputs needed

■ Exercise 1G (time: 30 minutes)

You have asked the local maternal and child health (MCH) coordinator to supply you with a list of the inputs to the MCH programme, which is one of the activities of your district. She has provided you with the following list. The programme carries out five activities: growth monitoring of 0–5-year-olds, treatment of common diseases in 0–5-year-olds, immunization, and prenatal and postnatal care. Here is her list of inputs.

● *Nurse.* The nurse is paid by the Ministry of Health (MOH). She takes part in all five activities.
● *Vaccine.* This is imported, and funds are supplied by a foreign aid agency. It is used for immunization only.
● *Refrigerator.* There is one kerosene-operated refrigerator for all the activities of the health centre to which the MCH centre is attached. This was purchased from abroad five years ago by the MOH. Drugs and vaccines for treatment, immunization and prenatal/postnatal care are stored in it.
● *Bicycles.* The health centre staff use two bicycles to visit patients who live nearby. About half of this use is by the MCH nurse. One bicycle was purchased from a local manufacturer by the MOH ten years ago (it is very

rickety now) and the other was supplied very recently by a foreign aid agency, and was manufactured in France.

- *Vehicle.* A small rough-terrain vehicle (purchased two years ago by the MOH from the United Kingdom) is used jointly by the MCH nurse and other health centre staff. The MCH nurse uses it to run a mobile child health clinic on Thursdays for growth monitoring and immunization.
- *Driver.* The driver is also shared with the other health centre activities and used on Thursdays for the mobile clinic. He is paid by the MOH.
- *Set of weighing scales.* These are used for growth monitoring. They were purchased from a local manufacturer using MOH funds.
- *Nurse-assistant.* The nurse-assistant is occupied in all activities and paid by the MOH.
- *Health centre premises.* The health centre building is used as an MCH clinic for half days totalling two days per week. It was built fifteen years ago, using mainly local materials, and was funded by the MOH.
- *Drugs.* Drugs are used for treatment and for prenatal and postnatal care. They are almost all imported and are funded by an international agency.
- *Beds.* All the health centre activities have access to two beds. These are used for deliveries or for sick children and their mothers. They were funded as part of the health centre building.
- *Syringes.* Syringes are used to administer both drugs and vaccines. They are purchased locally and funded by MOH.

What inputs has your MCH coordinator forgotten? List them below.

Classify all the inputs on the list above and those you have added by input category, by function (activity) and by source of funding. Put your answers below.

Input	Input category	Function	Source
Nurse			
Vaccine			
Refrigerator			
Bicycles			
Vehicle			
Driver			
Scales			
Nurse-assistant			
Premises			
Drugs			
Beds			
Syringes			

EXERCISES FOR MODULE 2

■ Exercise 2A (time: 45 minutes)

For your health programme (the one you used as an example for exercise 1B), compare what was spent with what was budgeted, both in total and for any specific programme function that you expect to be crucial, for the most recent available year.

Does your analysis show that budgeted values and expenditure have been well-matched (say, within 5% of each other) or not?

How could you improve the match between the budget and actual expenditure? (Take only about 15 minutes to tackle this question for purposes of an exercise.) Consider what new information, if any, you would need to answer that question. As part of your solution, would you:

- Change the objectives of the programme?   □ Yes   □ No
- Change the amounts allocated to the budget (increasing the amount provided by current sources or seeking alternative funds)?
  □ Yes   □ No
- Improve the efficiency of the programme?   □ Yes   □ No
  If yes, how?

- Incorporate more flexibility to deal with external developments genuinely outside your control and of an unpredictable nature? □ Yes   □ No

What else would you try to do?

Looking forward to larger analyses (during training exercises and after the course is over), here are (a) a suggested format for summarizing your budget and expenditure data and (b) some questions to ask. (There is no need to deal with them immediately.)

Input	Budget (currency ...)	Expenditure (currency ...)
Capital		
Vehicles		
Equipment		
Buildings, space		
Training, nonrecurrent		
Social mobilization, nonrecurrent		
Subtotal, capital		
Recurrent		
Personnel		
Supplies		
Vehicles, operation & maintenance		
Buildings, operation & maintenance		
Training, recurrent		
Social mobilization, recurrent		
Other operating inputs		
Subtotal, recurrent		
Total		

Questions to ask about your health programme include the following:

- Did total expenditure stay within the budget?
- Compared with previous years, are budgets and expenditures better matched?
- For which inputs was the budget overspent, and for which was it underspent?

Instead of "inputs" you could refer to donors, functions, currencies or levels. For each such classification, record the budget and expenditure, and then answer the following: for which donors/functions/currencies/levels was the budget overspent?

■ Exercise 2B (time: 15 minutes)

In a study of the costs of a disease control programme, you discover that all the health centres in your district, except one, devote between 5% and 8% of their total expenditure to drugs. The remaining centre devotes 20% of its resources to drugs. What are three possible explanations for this?

Explanation 1:

Explanation 2:

Explanation 3:

How would you go about deciding which one of these explanations is correct?

If explanation 1:

If explanation 2:

If explanation 3:

Consider what corrective action you would take in each case. (Do *not* write down your answers for this part.)

Now return to page 13 for some answers.

■ Exercise 2C (time: 30 minutes)

What is your programme's annual expenditure per person in the target population, divided between rural and urban areas?
Rural:

Urban:

If you had any serious difficulty making the above estimates, what kind(s) of information limitations made it difficult?

What factors might explain the differences that you might find between two districts in their cost (expenditure) per person for a certain set of services?

■ Exercise 2D (time: 2 hours — 1 hour for group work and 1 hour for groups to compare results)

A series of exercises based on tables similar to those provided in the final section of Module 2 is given below. It is recommended that students in a training course form four small groups of two or three people, and that each group does one or two exercises, as follows: group 1—exercise (a) (comparing districts); group 2—exercise (b) (for one district); group 3—exercises (c) and (d) (for one district); and group 4—exercises (e) (for one district) and (f) (for all levels).

The exercises are based on the tables at the end of Module 2, as follows:

- Exercise (a): Table 2.6
- Exercise (b): Table 2.1
- Exercise (c): Table 2.2
- Exercise (d): Table 2.3
- Exercise (e): Table 2.4
- Exercise (f): Table 2.5.

Exercise (a)—Expenditure by district

	District A		District B		District C		District D		Total	
Input	Currency	%	Currency	%	Currency	%	Currency	%	Currency	%
Capital										
Vehicles	20000		150000		25700		32500			
Equipment	10700		39600		14800		16300			
Buildings, space	11000		24660		10500		17500			
Training, nonrecurrent	0		0		0		0			
Social mobilization, nonrecurrent	0		0		0		0			
Subtotal, capital										
Recurrent										
Personnel	57900		124630		47800		76930			
Supplies	24600		50000		9240		33600			
Vehicles, operation & maintenance	12300		65000		5550		20700			
Buildings, operation & maintenance	2400		3750		2000		4070			
Training, recurrent	0		0		0		0			
Social mobilization, recurrent	0		0		0		0			
Other operating inputs	8750		20000		9860		13500			
Subtotal, recurrent										
Total	147650		477640		125450		214880			
Population served	50000		100000		40000		70000			

Calculate the percentage distribution of total cost (expenditure) among the input categories in each district, and enter your calculations in the "%" columns of the table.

Which districts have significantly different profiles and for which inputs?

What might account for these different cost profiles?

Calculate the cost per head (per capita cost) in each district, and put your results in a new row at the bottom of the table.

In which district is cost per head highest?

What might account for that?

Exercise (b)—Comparison of budget and expenditure, District A

Input	Budget (currency . . .)	Expenditure (currency . . .)	Cost profile (expenditure as % of budget)
Capital			
Vehicles	18 000	20 000	
Equipment	10 000	10 700	
Buildings, space	12 000	11 000	
Training, nonrecurrent	0	0	
Social mobilization, nonrecurrent	0	0	
Subtotal, capital			
Recurrent			
Personnel	60 000	57 900	
Supplies	20 000	24 600	
Vehicles, operation & maintenance	10 000	12 300	
Buildings, operation & maintenance	2700	2400	
Training, recurrent	0	0	
Social mobilization, recurrent	0	0	
Other operating inputs	9000	8750	
Subtotal, recurrent			
Total	141 700	147 650	

Complete the last column in the table.

Did the district's total expenditure keep within the budget (say, within 3–5% of it)?   ☐ Yes   ☐ No

Which inputs were overspent and which were underspent?

What percentage of total expenditure was on capital?

What are the recurrent cost implications of this capital expenditure?

For which inputs was expenditure greatest?

Might these be a focus for future efficiency studies? If so, how could such studies be carried out?

Exercise (c)—Expenditure by source of support (contributor), District A

Input	Donors		Ministry of Health		Other government departments		Total	
	Currency	%	Currency	%	Currency	%	Currency	%
Capital								
Vehicles	15000		5000		0		20000	
Equipment	6750		3250		700		10700	
Buildings, space	11000		0		0		11000	
Training, nonrecurrent	0		0		0		0	
Social mobilization, nonrecurrent	0		0		0		0	
Subtotal, capital								
Recurrent								
Personnel	0		49500		8400		57900	
Supplies	15000		9600		0		24600	
Vehicles, operation & maintenance	0		12300		0		12300	
Buildings, operation & maintenance	0		1800		600		2400	
Training, recurrent	0		0					
Social mobilization, recurrent	0		0					
Other operating inputs	0		6750		2000		8750	
Subtotal, recurrent								
Total	47750		88200		11700		147650	

(Note: These data assume *no* cost recovery through fees.)

What percentage of total cost (expenditure) of the district is provided by outside donors?

Which inputs are more dependent than others on outside donors?

For a district oriented towards primary health care, what kinds of supplies are most likely to be provided by outside donors?

Exercise (d)—Expenditure by type of currency, District A

Input	Donors		Ministry of Health		Other government departments		Total	
	Currency	%	Currency	%	Currency	%	Currency	%
Foreign exchange								
Capital inputs	30 000		1 700		550		32 250	
Recurrent inputs	15 000		22 000		500		37 500	
Subtotal	45 000		23 700		1 050		69 750	
Local currency								
Capital	2 750		4 500		2 200		9 450	
Recurrent	0		60 000		8 450		68 450	
Subtotal	2 750		64 500		10 650		77 900	
Total	47 750		88 200		11 700		147 650	

(Note: These data assume *no* cost recovery through fees.)

What percentage of total cost (expenditure) involves foreign exchange?

Which contributors provide most of the foreign exchange?

Are capital or recurrent inputs more dependent on foreign exchange?

What kinds of capital inputs are likely to be dependent on foreign exchange?

Exercise (e)—Expenditure by function (activity), District A

Input	Training		Management		Delivery		Education		Total	
	Currency	%	Currency	%	Currency	%	Currency	%	Currency	%
Capital										
Vehicles	3 000		1 200		6 800		9 000		20 000	
Equipment	900		600		7 300		1 900		10 700	
Buildings, space	500		500		9 500		500		11 000	
Training, nonrecurrent	0		0		0		0		0	
Social mobilization, nonrecurrent	0		0		0		0		0	
Subtotal, capital										
Recurrent										
Personnel	7 000		2 900		40 000		8 000		57 900	
Supplies	1 500		1 000		17 500		4 600		24 600	
Vehicles, operation & maintenance	1 900		750		4 200		5 450		12 300	
Buildings, operation & maintenance	100		100		2 100		100		2 400	
Training, recurrent	0		0		0		0		0	
Social mobilization, recurrent	0		0		0		0		0	
Other operating inputs	750		500		6 000		1 500		8 750	
Subtotal, recurrent										
Total	15 650		7 550		93 400		31 050		147 650	

Which functions (activities) are most capital-intensive (i.e. require a high percentage of capital inputs)?

On which function is expenditure highest?

Does that function give you the most scope for improving efficiency? Why/why not?

Exercise (f)—Expenditure by level, District A

Input	National administration		Regional administration		District administration		Health centre		Hospital		Total	
	Currency	%	Currency	%	Currency	%	Currency	%	Currency	%	Currency	%
Capital												
Vehicles	10		10		10		280		500			
Equipment	15		10		5		175		500			
Buildings, space	125		113		70		90		675			
Training, nonrecurrent	0		0		0		0		0			
Social mobilization, nonrecurrent	0		0		0		0		0			
Subtotal, capital												

Recurrent

Personnel	450	275	200	4500	3760
Supplies	10	7	5	1200	1350
Vehicles, operation & maintenance	10	10	10	375	200
Buildings, operation & maintenance	30	20	10	100	400
Training, recurrent					
Social mobilization, recurrent					
Other operating inputs	5	5	5	150	350
Subtotal, recurrent					
Total	655	450	315	6870	7735

At which level are most of the costs (expenditure) incurred?

At which level is the percentage of expenditure on capital inputs the highest?

EXERCISES FOR MODULE 3

■ Exercise 3A (time: 15 minutes)

What kind of sampling (that is, which of the approaches to sampling described in Module 3) would you adopt if you wanted to estimate as accurately as possible the average costs of certain services at health centres throughout your country?

What would be your second choice for the kind of sampling in the case above?

Briefly state the relative merits of the two choices.

Are you able to use your expenditure records to prepare a cost profile of inputs for your programme—as outlined in Module 2—or do the records need to be redesigned for that purpose? If so, how?

In view of the various kinds of information needed and tables of results planned for the costs of your programme, what changes, if any, would you propose for the existing expenditure records?

■ Exercise 3B (time: 45 minutes)

What is the most recent year for which you have expenditure records for your programme?

In your opinion, is that a recent enough year for which to make useful cost calculations for your programme?   ☐ Yes   ☐ No

Do the available expenditure records apply only to your programme (i.e. they contain no data applying to other programmes)?   ☐ Yes   ☐ No

If they contain data from other programmes, is this a serious problem? Why?

Are records available for expenditure supported by *all* the contributors to your programme, or only for the expenditure supported by certain contributors? If only certain ones, which ones?

EXERCISES FOR MODULE 4

■ Exercise 4A (time: 40 minutes)

What kinds of data exist on the nature and costs of the personnel used in your programme, and where can these data be found (and at what levels)?

What kinds?	Where?

Do these data identify the specific personnel and their work time (for costs) associated with your particular programme alone, or will some sort of distribution (allocation) of their costs among several programmes be required?

Are there any personnel involved in your programme whose costs are not included in the usual sources? If so, who are they?

What fringe (additional) benefits or allowances do your staff members (of all kinds) receive? For each of these, where, specifically, would you expect to find the information to estimate their value (cost)?

Benefits	Sources of information

■ Exercise 4B (time: 20 minutes)

List up to five major types of supplies required for your programme, and for each type indicate the most likely source(s) of data on the quantity used.

Type	Sources

Are these data likely to be detailed enough for the purposes of a cost study?
  □ Yes   □ No

Are any types of supplies shared with other programmes, and if so, how might you separate your programme's use from the rest?

Where can you get the most accurate data on the prices paid for these types of supplies or (better) their replacement prices?

Type	Source of price data

■ Exercise 4C (time: 15 minutes)

What sources of data exist on the costs of operating and maintaining vehicles for your programme, and at what level can you find them?

Source	Level

Are these data likely to be good enough for you to use in estimating the operation and maintenance costs of vehicles?

☐ Yes ☐ No

If not, what is the most promising source of information for estimating these costs?

■ Exercise 4D (time: 1 hour 15 minutes)

The following represents the total expenditure recorded for the last year for each of the inputs of a maternal and child health (MCH) programme. Examine the list and answer the questions.

Input	Expenditure (local currency)
Nurse	900
Vaccine	5000
Refrigerator	0
Bicycles	0
Car	0
Driver	600
Scales	0
Nurse assistant	700
Health centre (building)	0
Drugs	10000
Syringes	1000
Fuel	3000

What additional information will you need to assign each of these expenditures to the MCH programme's activities: (a) growth monitoring of 0–5-year-olds; (b) treatment of common diseases in 0–5-year-olds; (c) immunization; (d) prenatal and postnatal care?

For example, for capital costs you need to know the current price of each item and its expected useful life. Assume that these are:

- Refrigerator: 10-year lifetime, current price $800.
- Bicycle: 10-year lifetime, current price $200.
- Car: 8-year lifetime, current price $20000.
- Scales: 25-year lifetime, current price $100.
- Health centre building: 30-year lifetime, current cost of construction $15000.

Which of the inputs in the original table can be assigned directly to a particular MCH activity? (Match each such input with the activity.)

Input	Activity

For each of the remaining inputs—that is, those that cannot be directly assigned and so will require allocation of their costs among activities—suggest what component you would use to allocate their costs.

Input	Component

Assume that you now have the following additional information:

- The nurse and nurse assistant spend approximately equal time on all five MCH activities.
- The volume of drugs is approximately three times that of vaccine, and one-third of the drugs must be stored in the refrigerator. Half of the drugs (by volume) are used for treatment of common diseases in 0–5-year-olds, and one-quarter each for prenatal and postnatal care.
- The mobile child health clinic (which provides outreach services equally for all MCH functions except prenatal and postnatal care) accounts for 10% of the time for which the car and driver are used.

Which input costs are still difficult to allocate? What assumed cost values will you allocate to them, and why, in the absence of more information?

Input	Allocated costs

Now, summarize the annual costs—based on assigned and allocated expenditure and any other relevant calculation by you—for each of the original inputs and for the total. Show your calculations.

Input	Annual cost	Calculation (if needed)
Nurse		
Vaccine		
Refrigerator		
Bicycles		
Car		
Driver		
Scales		
Nurse assistant		
Health centre (building)		
Drugs		
Syringes		
Fuel		

EXERCISES FOR MODULE 5

■ Exercise 5A (time: 30 minutes)

If you want to compare the efficiency of operation of your programme at different health facilities (or different villages), what measures of effectiveness could you choose? Which single measure do you think would be the most satisfactory? (Indicate that one by an asterisk (∗).)

Suppose you are responsible for malaria control and have narrowed the choice down to household spraying or environmental management to control mosquitos. If you were to do a cost-effectiveness analysis of these alternatives, what measure of effectiveness would you choose, and why?

Suppose you are wondering whether to invest more money in diarrhoea control or in malaria control and you decide to do a cost-effectiveness analysis. What measure of effectiveness would you choose?

What other factors—apart from the cost-effectiveness results of your diarrhoea-versus-malaria comparison—do you think you would need to consider in making your decision about the choice of investment?

■ Exercise 5B (time: 15 minutes)

Can you think of any side-effects of vector control programmes that are not included in the effectiveness measure "reduction in vector density"? Name any important ones.

Which of these side-effects are likely to be important for an insecticide spraying programme?

■ Exercise 5C (time: 30 minutes)

An education programme to persuade women in hospital to breast-feed their babies involves several steps. Starting with the provision of a staff educator, describe briefly what you think these steps would be.

What might the immediate services be?

What might be the intermediate effects and the long-term health status effects? How would you measure each of these outputs?

Intermediate

Effect	Measure

Long-term

Effect	Measure

■ Exercise 5D (time: 1 hour 15 minutes)

Consider the following indicators of effectiveness for various PHC programmes, and classify each as: (a) immediate service *or* (b) effect on knowledge, attitudes and practices (KAP) *or* (c) impact on health status.

Indicator	Classification (a, b or c)
number of children weighed	
incidence of water-borne diseases	
number of under-fives vaccinated	
number of people using latrines	
number of health education meetings held	
maternal deaths	
infant deaths	
number of prenatal sessions held	
number of couples using contraceptives	
number of immunization sessions held	
tetanus mortality	
measles mortality	
number of contraceptives distributed	
number of mothers breast-feeding after six months	
number of children on supplementary feeding	
amount of vitamin A distributed	
number of deliveries attended	
number of women receiving tetanus toxoid immunizations	
number of radio spots for health education	
number of pit latrines dug	
number of water sources provided	
number of deaths from tetanus	
number of malnourished children	

Pick *three* of the indicators of effectiveness from the list on p. 124 and try to think
of two ways of influencing each of them (for example, if you select "number of
deaths from tetanus", you could consider tetanus toxoid immunization and
training of traditional birth attendants).

Measure	Two ways to influence it	
	1)	2)
	1)	2)
	1)	2)

For each of the three measures you have chosen, discuss briefly its suitability as a
basis for comparing the effectiveness of alternative activities.

Measure	Suitability
1.	
2.	
3.	

EXERCISE FOR MODULE 6

■ Exercise 6A (time: 15 minutes)

The objectives of the malaria control programme are assumed to be reductions in morbidity and mortality from that disease. Listed below are some of the specific functions (activities) of the programme and certain inputs needed for each function. (Do not worry about adding inputs or functions which have been omitted.) For each function, give three measures of unit cost that you think would be useful; the first answers have already been provided for your guidance.

Subprogramme	Function	Inputs	Unit cost measure
Prevention	Vector control	Sprayers, insec-ticide, vehicles	Cost per house sprayed
			Cost per person protected
			Cost per case prevented
	Chemoprophy-laxis	Staff, drugs, building	
Treatment	Prescription and related care	Staff, drugs	
	Rehabilitation	Staff, bednets, repellent	
Central support	National (or regional or dis-trict) laboratory	Staff, slides, microscopes	

■ Exercise 7A (time: 15 minutes)

What kinds of resource inputs are provided "free" or at a discount to your programme? For each of these, what approach would you use to determine its economic cost?

Input	Approach
	a)
	b)
	a)
	b)
	a)
	b)

Does the market price of any of these inputs fail to reflect its true value? If so, why?

■ Exercise 7B (time: 30 minutes)

A health centre has the following vehicles fully assigned to it: one ambulance with a replacement cost of $7000; one four-wheel-drive vehicle with a cost of $15 000; and 10 bicycles with a cost of $100 each. Assume useful lives for these vehicles as follows: ambulance, 10 years; four-wheel-drive vehicle, 8 years; bicycles, 2 years. Use a discount rate of 6%. What is the total annualized capital cost of the vehicles?

Ambulance: $7000/_____ = $_____ per year

Four-wheel-drive vehicle: $15 000/_____ = $_____ per year

Each bicycle: $100/_____ = $_____per year, so 10 bicycles = $_____ per year

Total annualized capital cost of vehicles = $_____ per year

■ Exercise 7C (time: 45 minutes)

Refer back to exercise 4D, which provided data for calculating the *financial* costs of an MCH programme. Now, you wish to estimate the *economic* costs of the programme. The following information should help you:

- The wages paid in the private sector for nurses and for nurse assistants are $1350 and $1050 per year, respectively.
- The driver's wage is the official national minimum, but in the informal sector drivers are paid only $300 per year.
- There is always a shortage of fuel in the official markets, and on the black market the price is about four times the official price.
- The official rate of exchange is 50 shillings = US$1, but on the black market the average rate is 250 shillings = US$1 (note: this means that the economic cost of all imported items is five times the official price).
- The discount rate used by the national planning office is 8%.
- Data on almost all capital items, such as vehicles and large items of equipment, are given in excercise 4D, page 119. For building space, use the equivalent of US$300 per year (which treats space, in effect, as a recurrent cost).

Calculate the annual *economic* costs of the programme, entering your results in the table on the next page, which gives the standard input categories. For each category, indicate also the *financial* costs that you estimated in Exercise 4D. Show all necessary calculations for the economic costs, indicating clearly the factors you have taken into account.

Input	Economic cost (local currency)	Financial cost (local currency)
Capital		
Vehicles		
Equipment		
Buildings, space		
Training, nonrecurrent		
Social mobilization, nonrecurrent		
Subtotal, capital		
Recurrent		
Personnel		
Supplies		
Vehicles, operation & maintenance		
Buildings, operation & maintenance		
Training, recurrent		
Social mobilization, recurrent		
Other operating inputs		
Subtotal, recurrent		
Total		

EXERCISES FOR MODULE 8

■ Exercise 8A (time: 30 minutes)

For your programme, what are the major kinds of costs incurred by households that use your services?

What could be done, if anything, to reduce any of the costs? Comment on each of the costs you have identified, and note which of the measures intended to reduce household costs would *create* costs for your programme (at any level).

● Exercise 8B (time: 60 minutes)

A household survey has been carried out in your district and has classified people as "frequent attenders" (those who have visited government health facilities more than twice in the past year) and "infrequent attenders" (those who have visited less than twice). The table below gives some data for the two groups.

Data on household and its health contacts	Frequent attenders	Infrequent attenders
Average distance to government facility (km)	5.1	7.5
Average distance to closest nongovernment facility (km)	10.5	9.9
Average waiting time at last government clinic visit (min)	48	63
Average fee paid at government clinic	0.1	0.12
Average amount spent on drugs related to last visit	1.8	1.7
Average no. of rooms in house	1.4	1.2
Average annual household income	243	198
Average no. of persons in household	6.8	6.6

From the survey information, what factors appear to be most important in *deterring* utilization?

If average speed of travel is 5 km per hour, what are the approximate time costs per visit to the government facility, for each group? (Remember that each patient must make both an outward and a return journey. Ignore for the moment the relatives or other persons who accompany patients, even though this will mean that you underestimate the total household travel time.)

Frequent attenders:

Infrequent attenders:

What costs to the households cannot be calculated from the above information?

What percentage of household income would actually be spent on health services if each household member made two visits to the nearest government health facility each year? In your opinion, are these services affordable? Why, or why not?

Percentage of income spent:

Affordable?

Why?

EXERCISES FOR MODULE 9

■ Exercise 9A (time: 20 minutes)

What are the principal objectives of your programme?

Are there any specific aspects of the programme over which you have control? What are they? Indicate the main objectives of each.

Aspect	Objectives

Write down three problems that exist in your programme. Re-express each problem as a desired objective.

Problem	Objective

■ Exercise 9B (time: 20 minutes)

Select one of the problems in your programme that you identified in exercise 9A. Identify up to five different solutions to help you meet the objective. Be imaginative.

The problem:

Possible solutions:

Which of these solutions are likely to survive testing against the four points about eliminating options listed on pages 69–70?

● Exercise 9C (time: 20 minutes)

You discover that someone in another country is running a similar programme to yours, namely educating mothers delivering in hospital with the objective of increasing rates of breast-feeding. You wish to compare the two programmes. For each hospital you measure the costs and estimate the number of additional women breast-feeding. You find that in the first hospital costs are $1.00 per woman breast-feeding (who would not otherwise have breast-fed) and in the second hospital costs are $0.50.

What could be the causes of this difference? Structure your answer to consider these factors: (i) educational technique; (ii) prices; (iii) hospital size; (iv) characteristics of women; (v) other factors. For each cause, state whether you could influence it.

Factor	Can you influence it?

■ Exercise 9D (time: 30 minutes)

Two methods have been identified for administration of tetanus toxoid. Toxoid can be given routinely, as part of the regular prenatal care activities of the MCH clinic, or special campaigns can be mounted occasionally with mobile units aiming to immunize all eligible women in the district.

The costs and some indicators of effectiveness for the two methods are given in the table below.

Cost item	Routine	Campaign
Health units	17 000	15 600
Management	3 500	7 600
Vaccines	1 250	1 600
Publicity	0	2 400
Vehicles	250	2 400
Capital items	2 250	2 800
Other	750	4 000
Total	25 000	40 000
Number of immunizations	22 000	45 000
Number of women receiving at least two doses	8 000	10 000
Estimated reduction in number of deaths from neonatal tetanus	40	50

Which one of the effectiveness measures is most useful, and why?

Using the measure chosen for its usefulness, what are the cost-effectiveness ratios for the two methods (routine and campaign), and which method would be selected on the basis of that ratio? Show your calculations.

What considerations have been ignored in this calculation?

You are not sure about the cost of vaccine in the "campaign" option, because it is not currently in operation and you are not sure about relative wastage rates. They could be as much as double, or as little as half of the expected rates. Does this make any difference to the cost-effectiveness conclusions? Show any calculations.

What factors appear to be responsible for the difference in cost-effectiveness between the two methods? Does this suggest any possible modifications to the designs of the methods?

Factors:

Any modifications:

EXERCISES FOR MODULE 10

■ Exercise 10A (time: 15 minutes)

What are the principal difficulties that you can foresee in the "ingredients" approach (see page 78)?

In view of the probable strengths and weaknesses of the approach, in which cases do you think it would be most appropriate to use it?

If you had to list all the resources that you expected to use over the next year for a programme (regardless of the approach you might use for cost estimation for budget-making), which categories of resource inputs would be most difficult to quantify?

■ Exercise 10B (time: 1 hour 15 minutes)

A new training programme for community health workers (CHWs) is proposed in your district. It is planned to train 20 workers a year. Make a list of the inputs that will be required. Indicate the ones for which it will be difficult to make estimates in advance.

Suppose you have the following information from a neighbouring district which has already started its training programme (the costs apply to the previous year). It is training 30 CHWs per year. Costs include allocations of shared costs.

Inputs	Costs (local currency)
Capital	
Vehicles	600
Equipment	180
Building, space	100
Recurrent	
Personnel	1 400
Supplies	300
Vehicles, operation	380
Building, operation	20
Other operating inputs	150

Use these costs to estimate the costs of your programme for the next five years. Remember to include only those costs that are incremental, and to take account of the different sizes of the two programmes. Assume that inflation will be 10% per year. Use your answers to fill in the table below, and show all calculations.

Inputs	Year 1	Year 2	Year 3	Year 4	Year 5
Capital					
Vehicles					
Equipment					
Building, space					
Recurrent					
Personnel					
Supplies					
Vehicles, operation					
Building, operation					
Other operating inputs					

Calculations

The government estimate for training CHWs is $1500 per district per year. Is your proposal affordable? If it is not affordable, what suggestions could you make?

Is it affordable?   ☐ Yes   ☐ No

Show your calculation.

Suggestions (if necessary):

Calculate the cost per CHW trained during the first year of the new programme in your district.

What other measures of effectiveness might you use for this programme?

EXERCISES FOR MODULE 11

■ Exercise 11A (time: 30 minutes)

Refer back to exercise 2C. Assuming for your programme that you found some difference between rural and urban area groups in your population with respect to annual expenditure per person, what does that tell you about the geographical equity of the programme?

What other important measures of programme equity would you want to use, and how readily available are the data on each?

Measure of equity	Availability of data

■ Exercise 11B (time: 30 minutes)

Refer to exercise 10B. What, if anything, do your results concerning cost per CHW trained suggest about the equity of the training scheme?

Identify the most useful specific kinds of information that you would need in order to evaluate thoroughly the training scheme's equity and state very briefly why each is needed. (To help you: among other things, consider what happens after the training is over.)

■ Exercise 11C (time: 30 minutes)

In exercise 10B, you were told that the government had estimated its capacity to afford the training scheme for CHWs at $1500 per district per annum.

Briefly summarize the major elements that probably went into making that estimate.

What, if anything, could you do at the *district* level to help to make the training more affordable?

EXERCISE FOR MODULE 12

■ Exercise 12A (time: 30 minutes)

An economic study of the immunization programme in a country showed the following results for the average cost per vaccine dose and the average number of immunizations per session at five comparable delivery facilities. (More sites were studied, but are omitted here to keep the exercise short. Assume that their results would not change the overall results.)

Facility	Average no. of immunizations per session	Cost per dose (local currency)
A	40	2.30
B	50	1.80
C	120	0.90
D	180	0.60
E	220	0.40

What conclusion do you draw from these data about the relationships between average cost and intensity of use of facility capacity?

On the basis of these results (assuming that they really come from *many* typical facilities), what might be one or two policy implications for deployment of staff (e.g. where they are placed and when they are used)?

Suppose that someone recommends to you that you should provide immunization services in fewer but larger PHC facilities in your country in order to promote efficiency. What might be some of the major positive and negative factors that you would explore when considering that policy recommendation?

Annualization factors

Discount rate

Expected useful life in years	1%	2%	3%	4%	5%	6%	7%	8%	9%	10%	11%	12%	13%	14%	15%	16%	17%	18%	19%	20%
1	0.990	0.980	0.971	0.962	0.952	0.943	0.935	0.926	0.917	0.909	0.901	0.893	0.885	0.877	0.870	0.862	0.855	0.847	0.840	0.833
2	1.970	1.942	1.913	1.886	1.859	1.833	1.808	1.783	1.759	1.736	1.713	1.690	1.668	1.647	1.626	1.605	1.585	1.566	1.547	1.528
3	2.941	2.884	2.829	2.775	2.723	2.673	2.624	2.577	2.531	2.487	2.444	2.402	2.361	2.322	2.283	2.246	2.210	2.174	2.140	2.106
4	3.902	3.808	3.717	3.630	3.546	3.465	3.387	3.312	3.240	3.170	3.102	3.037	2.974	2.914	2.855	2.798	2.743	2.690	2.639	2.589
5	4.853	4.713	4.580	4.452	4.329	4.212	4.100	3.993	3.890	3.791	3.696	3.605	3.517	3.433	3.352	3.274	3.199	3.127	3.058	2.991
6	5.795	5.601	5.417	5.242	5.076	4.917	4.767	4.623	4.486	4.355	4.231	4.111	3.998	3.889	3.784	3.685	3.589	3.498	3.410	3.326
7	6.728	6.472	6.230	6.002	5.786	5.582	5.389	5.206	5.033	4.868	4.712	4.564	4.423	4.288	4.160	4.039	3.922	3.812	3.706	3.605
8	7.652	7.325	7.020	6.733	6.463	6.210	5.971	5.747	5.535	5.335	5.146	4.968	4.799	4.639	4.487	4.344	4.207	4.078	3.954	3.837
9	8.566	8.162	7.876	7.435	7.108	6.802	6.515	6.247	5.995	5.759	5.537	5.328	5.132	4.946	4.772	4.607	4.451	4.303	4.163	4.031
10	9.471	8.983	8.530	8.111	7.722	7.360	7.024	6.710	6.418	6.145	5.889	5.650	5.426	5.216	5.019	4.833	4.659	4.494	4.339	4.192
11	10.368	9.787	9.253	8.760	8.306	7.887	7.499	7.139	6.805	6.495	6.207	5.938	5.687	5.453	5.234	5.029	4.836	4.656	4.486	4.327
12	11.255	10.575	9.954	9.385	8.863	8.384	7.943	7.536	7.161	6.814	6.492	6.194	5.918	5.660	5.421	5.197	4.988	4.793	4.611	4.439
13	12.134	11.348	10.635	9.986	9.394	8.853	8.358	7.904	7.487	7.103	6.750	6.424	6.122	5.842	5.583	5.342	5.118	4.910	4.715	4.533
14	13.004	12.106	11.296	10.563	9.899	9.295	8.745	8.244	7.786	7.367	6.982	6.628	6.302	6.002	5.724	5.468	5.229	5.008	4.802	4.611
15	13.865	12.849	11.938	11.118	10.380	9.712	9.108	8.559	8.061	7.606	7.191	6.811	6.462	6.142	5.847	5.575	5.324	5.092	4.876	4.675
16	14.718	13.578	12.561	11.652	10.838	10.106	9.447	8.851	8.313	7.824	7.379	6.974	6.604	6.265	5.954	5.668	5.405	5.162	4.938	4.730
17	15.562	14.292	13.166	12.166	11.274	10.477	9.763	9.122	8.544	8.022	7.549	7.120	6.729	6.373	6.047	5.749	5.475	5.222	4.990	4.775
18	16.398	14.992	13.754	12.659	11.690	10.828	10.059	9.372	8.756	8.201	7.702	7.250	6.840	6.467	6.128	5.818	5.534	5.273	5.033	4.812
19	17.226	15.678	14.324	13.134	12.085	11.158	10.336	9.604	8.950	8.365	7.839	7.366	6.938	6.550	6.198	5.877	5.584	5.316	5.070	4.843
20	18.046	16.351	14.877	13.590	12.462	11.470	10.594	9.818	9.129	8.514	7.963	7.469	7.025	6.623	6.259	5.929	5.628	5.353	5.101	4.870
21	18.857	17.011	15.415	14.029	12.821	11.764	10.836	10.017	9.292	8.649	8.075	7.562	7.102	6.687	6.312	5.973	5.665	5.384	5.127	4.891
22	19.660	17.658	15.937	14.451	13.163	12.042	11.061	10.201	9.442	8.772	8.176	7.645	7.170	6.743	6.359	6.011	5.696	5.410	5.149	4.909
23	20.456	18.292	16.444	14.857	13.489	12.303	11.272	10.371	9.580	8.883	8.266	7.718	7.230	6.792	6.399	6.044	5.723	5.432	5.167	4.925
24	21.243	18.914	16.936	15.247	13.799	12.550	11.469	10.529	9.707	8.985	8.348	7.784	7.283	6.835	6.434	6.073	5.746	5.451	5.182	4.937
25	22.023	19.523	17.413	15.622	14.094	12.783	11.654	10.675	9.823	9.077	8.422	7.843	7.330	6.873	6.464	6.097	5.766	5.467	5.195	4.948
26	22.795	20.121	17.877	15.983	14.375	13.003	11.826	10.810	9.929	9.161	8.488	7.896	7.372	6.906	6.491	6.118	5.783	5.480	5.206	4.956
27	23.560	20.707	18.327	16.330	14.643	13.211	11.987	10.935	10.027	9.237	8.548	7.943	7.409	6.935	6.514	6.136	5.798	5.492	5.215	4.964
28	24.316	21.281	18.764	16.663	14.898	13.406	12.137	11.051	10.116	9.307	8.602	7.984	7.441	6.961	6.534	6.152	5.810	5.502	5.223	4.970
29	25.066	21.844	19.188	16.984	15.141	13.591	12.278	11.158	10.198	9.370	8.650	8.022	7.470	6.983	6.551	6.166	5.820	5.510	5.229	4.975
30	25.808	22.396	19.600	17.292	15.372	13.765	12.409	11.258	10.274	9.427	8.694	8.055	7.496	7.003	6.566	6.177	5.829	5.517	5.235	4.979

Further reading

Guidelines and methods

EPICOST software for costing an immunization programme. Geneva, World Health Organization, 1989 (available on request from Global Programme for Vaccines, World Health Organization, 1211 Geneva 27, Switzerland).

Estimating costs for cost-effectiveness analysis: guidelines for managers of diarrhoeal diseases control programmes. Geneva, World Health Organization, 1988 (unpublished document, CDD/SER/88.3; available on request from Diarrhoeal Disease Control, World Health Organization, 1211 Geneva 27, Switzerland).

Expanded Programme on Immunization: costing guidelines. Geneva, World Health Organization, 1979 (unpublished document EPI/GEN/79.5; available on request from Global Programme for Vaccines, World Health Organization, 1211 Geneva 27, Switzerland).

Mills A. Economic evaluation of health programmes: application of the principles in developing centres. *World health statistics quarterly*, 1985, **38**: 368–382.

Reynolds J, Gaspari KC. *Cost effectiveness analysis.* Chevy Chase, MD, Center for Human Services, 1985 (Pricor Monograph Series No. 2).

Case studies

Berman PA. Cost analysis as a management tool for improving the efficiency of primary care: some examples from Java. *International journal of health planning and management*, 1986, **1**: 275–288.

Lerman SJ, Shepard DS, Cash R. Treatment of diarrhoea in children: what it costs and who pays for it. *Lancet*, 1985, **2**: 651–654.

Over M. The effect of scale on cost projections for a primary health care program in a developing country. *Social science and medicine*, 1986, **22**: 351–360.

Qualls N, Robertson RL. Potential use of cost analysis in child survival programmes: evidence from Africa. *Health policy and planning*, 1989, **4**: 50–61.

Robertson RL, Davis JH, Jobe K. Service volume and other factors affecting the cost of immunizations in The Gambia. *Bulletin of the World Health Organization*, 1984, **62**: 729–736.

Index